MONT BL___.

A COMEDY,

IN THREE ACTS,

BY

HENRY AND ATHOL MAYHEW.

(First produced at the Theatre Royal Haymarket, Whit Monday, May 25th, 1874.)

☞ *Part of the plot of this piece is derived from* "LE VOYAGE DE M. PERRICHON," *by* MM. E. LABICHE *et* E. MARTIN.

LONDON:
PRINTED FOR PRIVATE CIRCULATION.
1874.

(*All rights reserved.*)

N.B.—*All applications for permission to perform this piece to be addressed to* H. P. GRATTAN, ESQ., 24, GLOUCESTER CRESCENT, REGENT'S PARK, LONDON.

In the interest of creating a more extensive selection of rare historical book reprints, we have chosen to reproduce this title even though it may possibly have occasional imperfections such as missing and blurred pages, missing text, poor pictures, markings, dark backgrounds and other reproduction issues beyond our control. Because this work is culturally important, we have made it available as a part of our commitment to protecting, preserving and promoting the world's literature. Thank you for your understanding.

TO

RICHARD CARROL BARTON, ESQ.

THIS PLAY IS

DEDICATED

AS

A TRIBUTE OF RESPECT

BY

THE AUTHORS.

DRAMATIS PERSONÆ.

As produced at the Theatre Royal Haymarket, May 25th, 1874.

Dr. Majoribanks, M.D., F.R.S., &c., &c.	Mr. Chippendale.
Harold Majoribanks, St. John's Coll., Camb. (*his Son*)	" Kendall.
Young Lord Silverspoon (*an Eton Boy*) *	" Buckstone, Junr.*
The Earl of Osborne (*his Uncle and Guardian*)	" Braid.
Hon. Percy Centlivre, *late of Trin. Coll., Camb.* (*Son of the Earl*)	" Howe.
Mr. Chirpey (*Oil and Italian Warehouseman, of St. Mary Axe, Lond.*)	" Buckstone.
Captain Broadside (*late of the Royal Indian Navy*)	" Rogers.
Le Captaine Achille Fortinbras (*late of the 12me Zouaves*)	" T. S. Jerrold.
Herr Professor Windbeutel, Ph.D. (*of Jena Un.*)	" Everill.
M. Lavigne (*Landlord of "Le Lion d'Or,"* Chamouni)	" Osborne.
Fritz (*Head-Waiter at "Le Lion d'Or"*)	" Clark.
François (*Head-Guide*)	" Gordon.
Baptiste (*2nd Guide*)	" Rivers.
Town Crier	" Weathersby.
Mrs. Chirpey	Mrs. Chippendale.
Florence (*her Daughter*)	Miss Amy Roselle.
Miss Jytham (*her Companion*)	" Helen Massey.
Mme. Lavigne (*Landlady of "Le Lion d'Or"*)	Mrs. Weathersby.
1st Visitor	Miss Lillie Watkins.
Market-Woman	" Lewin.

Mdlle. at Hotel-Bureau, Chambermaid. Waiters. Guests, Travellers, *and* Valet. Guides. Porters, Postillion, Ostler, Boots, &c. Syndic, Gendarmes, Swiss Peasants *and* Villagers.

The piece produced under the superintendence of Mr. COE.

* This part was written for, and is intended to be played by, a young lady.

MONT BLANC.

ACT I.

IN THE GARDEN AND COURT-YARD OF HOTEL AT CHAMOUNI.

SCENE.—*Exterior of "Le Lion d'Or" at Chamouni. The Flat represents the façade of the ground-floor and "entresol" of the Hotel. It has three long French windows in it, practicable, and opening down to the ground. All of these are thrown back, and through these is seen the "*SALLE À MANGER*" (the words of which are painted up in gold letters over the central casement), with the* TABLE D'HÔTE *going on within at the rising of the curtain.* GUESTS *seen seated at the table, and* WAITERS *rushing about to serve them.*

Entrance to Hotel in flat at R., with the figure of a GOLDEN LION *over the doorway, and the words "* LE LION D'OR *" printed in gold underneath it. Large flower-vases on either side of the door, and a barometer hanging up against one of the door posts. The entrance is left open, and a spacious Hall, with large lamp in it, seen behind, with board covered with numbers and keys hanging beneath some of the figures, and with stall of soap, set out with eau-de-Cologne and Swiss knick-knacks, alpenstocks, &c., on R. side of it.*

Above the French windows in the façade is arranged a long striped awning, with "built-out" balcony and practicable window in "flat" over this; and there are little round marble-topped coffee-tables, with rustic chairs, placed at intervals under the awning.

In front, the stage represents a parterre, with a large raised oval flower-bed made out upon it; this is bordered with coloured illumination-lamps and with orange-trees in square green boxes, and more little marble-topped tables and rustic chairs set out between them. A long rustic seat is arranged at R. and cannon at L.

On either side of the stage, the wings are closed in with a flat as far as first entrance—the one at R. representing the "Hotel-Bureau," with the word " BUREAU *" painted over the bay-window—and L. 1 E. closed in with gates between a pair of pillars—while the other flat closing in L. side represents the Hotel Stables, with the word "* REMISE *" over the door, which is practicable, and with a pump, which is also practicable, standing against the wall.*

Gate-bell rings violently without as curtain goes up.

Enter M. and MME. LAVIGNE *rushing out of Hotel-door at R. U. E. They stand on the steps as they shout off.*

M. LAVIGNE (*looking off* L.) Here, Fritz! Alphonse! Carlo!
MME. L. Gretchen! come!
M. LAVIGNE. Come all of you!
MME. L. (*ringing house-bell impatiently and calling into Hall*). Quick! The car from Sallenches has arrived!
M. LAVIGNE (*clapping his hands*). To the gate—stir yourselves.

Enter FRITZ, WAITERS, CHAMBERMAIDS, BOOTS, *and* GUIDES *hurriedly—some with napkins under their arms—through the open window* IN C. *leading to* TABLE D'HÔTE, *others by the Hotel-door at* R. U. E., *and the* OSTLER *from the Stables at* L.

All exeunt, running off, at L. 1 E.

GUESTS (*within at* TABLE D'HÔTE). Donner Wetter, Kellner!—Garçon, Sapristi! Hang it, Waitah!

Enter CAPTAIN BROADSIDE *through open window at* C. *He has a dinner napkin tucked under his chin, and holds the* WINE-CARTE *in one hand and a silver fork, with the leg of a fowl stuck on it, in the other.*

CAPTAIN B. (*coming down*). May I eat nothing but lobscouse for the rest of my days! if this isn't enough to turn all one's milk of human kindness into curds and whey. (*He eyes, disgustedly, the morsel at the end of his fork.*)

MME. L. For what does Monsieur incommode himself.

CAPTAIN B. Who the deuce wouldn't be incommoded, Madam? having to stand still in the middle of dinner like this—with one's leg in one's hand?

M. LAVIGNE. But what does Monsieur desire?

CAPTAIN B. Why, simply something to eat, Sir, and somebody to serve it, and be—no, damn it! I won't swear; or I shall lose, not only my temper, but my appetite (*puts leg of fowl down on table*).

M. LAVIGNE. Pardon! Here come the fresh arrivals.

Enter FRITZ, WAITERS, CHAMBERMAIDS, GUIDES, *and* PORTERS *with luggage, bowing in* TRAVELLERS L. 1 E.

FRITZ (*as the party comes up the stage*). Par ici, Messieurs et Mesdames. Dis vay, Laties and Shentlemens! *Treden sie nahe, mein Herren und Damen!*

CAPTAIN B. That land-shark of a Head-waiter jabbers as many lingoes as a Ratcliffe Highway parrot. (*Crosses to* L.)

1st VISITOR. What a charming little Hotel—isn't it, Charles?—and so quiet, too, after the excitement of that dear, darling Geneva!

M. LAVIGNE (*bowing*). Welcome to Chamouni, gentlemen! The "GOLDEN LION" opens his arms to receive you.

CAPTAIN B. (*aside*). And his jaws to devour you!

MME. L. Any gentleman wishing to ascend the mountain will please to notify the same to Mdlle. at the "BUREAU." (*Points to office-window at* L.)

M. LAVIGNE. A party going up to-morrow. Prices very moderate. Guides of the greatest experience. (*Points to the* GUIDES *at* R., *who raise their hats.*)

TRAVELLERS *bow and exeunt with* PORTERS, WAITERS, &c., *as well as* M. *and* MME. LAVIGNE, R. U. E.—*the latter handing the* TRAVELLERS *their keys from off the board, as they pass through the Hall.*

FRITZ (*detaining one of the* TRAVELLERS). Englisher Shentlemens all-days need leedel zoab. Hotel, you know, Sare, don't find no zoab. I have verita-able "Browns Vindsors"—vare fine bouquet! vare goot market! (*runs and fetches a cake from stall inside Hotel-door.*)

CAPTAIN B. (*down* L). There's that infernal Ober-kellner soaping them over again (*to* TRAVELLER, *as* FRITZ *takes the tin-foil off the cake, and puts the soap under the Gent's nose for him to smell*). Don't have it, Sir! Make 'em find it for you, Sir! Haul away at the bells till you get it, Sir.

Act I.   MONT BLANC.   7

FRITZ. Englisher Shentlemens all-days neet *Eau de Cologne*—of de first kallitay (*produces a bottle from the box he has brought with the soap, and makes* TRAVELLER *smell it*). Verita-able Yean Maria Farina! Vare fine bouquet! vare goot market!

CAPTAIN B. Bilge water, by Davy Jones, Sir! Don't have it, Sir! Outrageous imposition! nothing but imposition abroad, Sir!

TRAVELLER *shakes his head and exit* R. U. E.

FRITZ (*appealingly*). But, mein Herr Capitaine, vhy for you poke your nose in mine Eau de Cologne?

CAPTAIN B. Vhy for you spoil mine dinner? Look at this, you abandoned son of a sea cook (*thrusting fork close to his face*)! It's as raw as a cab-horse's knees!

FRITZ. But Monsieur le Capitaine say to me make von devil of him. Devil! How can be poseeble to make von devil of von leedel schicken! Vat devil you mean?

CAPTAIN B. And d'ye think I'm going to eat it as it is? No! Devil a bit of it (*he throws fork at* FRITZ's *head, and the wine-carte after it, as the latter exit through the open window at* C. *He then takes off napkin and wipes his forehead with it*). Phe-ew! this kind of treatment at dinner is enough to make the blood of a periwinkle boil. If I don't write to "THE TIMES" about it, I'm a Dutchman. And stop my grog! but I'll do it while the fit's on me too. Here, Kellner! Garçong! (*He takes up hand-bell from one of the marble-topped tables and rings it violently.*)

2ND WAITER *appears at the open French window at* C.

Apportez a sheet of *papier aux lettres*—letter paper—*brief-papyeer! Comprenez-vous?—verstehens sie?* D'ye understand?

WAITER *nods assent, bows, and exit* C.

Hang me! if one ha'n't to speak as many languages out here as if you'd taken apartments in the Tower of Babel. (*Crosses to table* R.)

WAITER *returns* L. U. E., *and, having placed writing materials on table at* R., *exit* L. U. E.

(*Sitting down to table, and taking up pen*). And now to let the enemy have it — grape and canister! (*writing*) "TO THE EDITOR OF THE TIMES. SIR,"—That I think will riddle their sails for them! (*continuing to write*) "*Knowing your columns to be always open*"—Avast heaving mate! Hadn't you better take a round turn there till you've been and shinned up to the truck of Mont Blanc? Ay! ay, Sir! round turn 'tis! Well said, Captain Broadside! Tip us your fin (*rises and shakes hands with himself*). I'm pleased to know you, Sir! and, if you find out the pirates here sailing under false colours, you're not the man I take you for if you don't blaze away at 'em with a red-hot twenty-four pounder—in the regular old-fashioned style of:—"TO THE EDITOR OF THE TIMES, SIR,—*Knowing your columns to be.*"

Exit CAPTAIN BROADSIDE C.

Gate-bell rings without. Enter M. LAVIGNE R. U. E.

M. LAVIGNE (*rubbing his hands as he stands on doorstep*). More arrivals! Ha! ha! The harvest goes well!

Enter DR. MAJORIBANKS, *followed by* PORTER, *who wears a cap with the name of the Hotel inscribed on the band of it, and carries portmanteau on his shoulder, and carpet-bag in his hand.*

M. LAVIGNE (*to* PORTER, *after slyly eyeing the labels on the luggage*). Chamber No. 23.   *Exit* PORTER R. 2 E

8   MONT BLANC.   Act I.

(*To* Dr. M.). Monsieur the Doctor comes may-be to make the ascent. Mountain air very bracing. Prices very moderate. Guides of the greatest experience!

Dr. M. No! no! I leave that to younger and stronger constitutions. Many English, and any illness here? Drains seem to be in good order (*sniffs and crosses to* C.). I can detect no noxious gases in the atmosphere (*goes sniffing about*).

M. Lavigne. Monsieur desires something to eat and to drink after his journey from the baths of St. Gervais. Our *table d'hôte* is only at its fourth course.

Dr. M. Immediately after travelling I never tax the digestive organs with a heavy meal. Let me have a basin of Julienne, some black bread, and a bottle of Vichy water—the "Haute Rive" spring if you have it; and served out here. Can't have too much of such air; it's the finest possible medicine. (*Goes to table* R.)

M. Lavigne. Yes! it's better and cheaper than the stuff *you* deal in. (*Aside as exit* C.)

The Doctor *goes and potters about. He pours out a glass of water from one of the carafons on the marble tables—eyes it—tastes it—and shakes his head after it. He then proceeds to the barometer, hanging beside the Hotel-door, taps at the glass, and makes a note in his note-book as to the height of the mercury. And while the* Waiter *is laying the cloth he takes up the black bread, smells it, tastes it, and nods his head approvingly, as he smacks his lips, at the quality of it.*

Enter the Earl of Osborne, *in a light dust-coat, followed by* Valet, *and* Postillion *in high jack-boots.*

Earl of O. (*as* Valet *helps him off with his dust-coat*). Glad you stopped that bell, Thompson. Might as well have out the town-crier to announce one's arrival.

Enter 2nd Waiter, *who proceeds to lay cloth on one of the small round tables at* L.

Pay the post-boy his course from St. Martin, Thompson, and his drink-money too (Valet *bows*), and order me a basin of Vermicelli, with some grated Parmesan, and half a-pint of their best Madeira. Say too, I'll take it out here. And remember, Thompson, not a word about who I am. Put me down in the "Travellers' Book" as plain Mr. Osborne, —*Rentier* of course—from Baden-Baden—going to—anywhere you like.

Valet *bows and exit with* Postillion L. U. E.

Dr. M. (*coming forward*). Baden-Baden! and that voice! Surely I, —Yes it is! By all that's agreeable and astonishing, the Earl of Osborne! (*Raises his hat, and drops his stethoscope from the inside of it.*)

Earl of O. Sh—sh Doctor! a little less of the Earl, if you please. When I wish my travels published as an "*Edition de Luxe*," I shall not object to your putting the *title* on the back. At present, however, I want to appear *unbound;* and, therefore, desire to sink the calf and gilt-lettering.

Waiter. The gentlemen are served. (*Pointing to table* L.)

Dr. M. And both at the same table! an unexpected honour and pleasure too.

They proceed to lunch—the Doctor *obsequiously placing the Earl's chair for him; and, when they are seated at the little round table, which is so small that their faces nearly meet over it, the* Waiter *raises the covers of the silver soup-basins, and exit* C.

Act I.   MONT BLANC.   9

Dr. M. (*as he keeps blowing away at a spoonful of the steaming potage*). And how—pooh! is the sciatica, my Lord—pooh! that is Mr. Osborne, I mean.

Earl of O. (*scalding himself*). Infernally hot! Oh, the sciatica!—much better, thanks! The mud-baths got rid of it—I was going to say, *clean ;* though that's hardly the expression, Doctor, for so dirty a remedy.

Dr. M. You go on with your quinine, and keep away from all stimulants.

Earl of O. (*who has poured out a glass of Madeira, and is about to put it to his lips, when he sees the Doctor staring in utter astonishment at what he is doing*). No, I'm hanged if I do! and so here goes (*drinks off the glass, and smacks his lips loudly after it*).

Dr. M. (*shrugging his shoulders*). Well, Mr. Osborne, you pay the penalty.

Earl of O. (*filling another glass and bowing to the Doctor as he raises it*). And you, Doctor, receive the fines.

They proceed to sip their soup, and to talk rapidly—with their faces nearly meeting over the table—between the mouthfuls.

Waiters *on and off during this scene.*

Dr. M. Mr. Osborne is never going to venture on the ascent?
Earl of O. Not I, indeed! And you, Doctor?
Dr. M. Nor I! I have come up here to look after a truant son of mine.
Earl of O. How odd! And I am here on the same errand.
Dr. M. But I thought the Hon. Mr. Centlivre was in training for a diplomatic life and always at his books—such a hard-working young man!
Earl of O. And I that Mr. Harold Majoribanks was in training for a seat in the Cambridge boat and always at his athletics—such a hard-walking young man!
Dr. M. But have you no suspicion, Mr. Osborne, as to the cause of the young gentleman's sudden disappearance?
Earl of O. Only the faintest surmise! And you, Doctor?
Dr. M. Merely the vaguest conjecture.
Earl of O. My idea, with regard to my son, is that there's a petticoat in the case.
Dr. M. I have the very same notion concerning mine.
Earl of O. My son met the girl at the *table d'hôte* at Baden-Baden.
Dr. M. And so did mine.
Earl of O. Used to go excursions with her upon donkeys into the Black Forest.
Dr. M. My boy did the donkey too.
Earl of O. Her governor, I hear, is some vulgar Oil and Italian Warehouseman.
Dr. M. So is the father of my son's charmer—sprung, one may say, from a mere mushroom *source !*
Earl of O. The pickling and preserving *parvenu !*
Dr. M. It must be the same. Father's name Chirpey—eh?
Earl of O. The identical euphonious patronymic!

They rise from the table simultaneously, and pace the stage in opposite directions.

Dr. M. The double-faced she-Janus. (*Takes stage* L.)
Earl of O. The smooth-faced Giovanni in petticoats. (*Takes stage* R.)

Dr. M. (*meeting the Earl in the middle of the stage*). Well, my Lord, both our sons can't marry the girl!

Earl of O. Certainly not. Our Social Grammar does not yet admit of such irregular conjugations.

Dr. M. I was therefore about to observe—

Earl of O. And I was just going to say—

Dr. M. and Earl of O. } (*as they shake hands and bow*). My son will be only too happy to give way to yours.

Dr. M. (*as about to retire* C). You're extremely good, my Lord, but I couldn t listen to such a proposal.

Earl of O. (*while going off at Bureau* R. 3 E.). Very kind of you, Doctor, but I'd never be party to any such arrangement. *Exeunt.*

Waiter enters and clears table at L.

Enter Young Lord Silverspoon R.C. *as if coming from the* Table d'Hôte. *He has a plate of iced pudding in one hand, and a spongecake, which he is nibbling at, in the other. He is followed by* Miss Jetsam, *who wears a large "flippertiflop" garden-hat, and carries a small watering-pot and set of gardening tools.*

Lord S. (*with a drawling, used-up air, and yawning, as he proceeds towards one of the coffee-tables at* L ; *and, having placed his iced-pudding upon it, throws himself into one chair, and puts his legs up, languidly, on another*). Oh, I say, Miss Jetsam! such an awfully jolly lark! (*yawns*) Really wakes one up a bit!

Miss Jetsam (*putting down her tools in front of one of the flowerbeds at* R, *and preparing to clip some of the plants*). Your Lordship is generally a little somnolent—especially after dinner.

Lord S. (*eating his ice*). Ye-es! (*yawns again*) Dr. Majoribanks—the crack-jaw old fogie—used to tell that antediluvian Governor of mine that my lardydardiness was owing to my—a—a (*imitating the Doctor's manner*) " su-perfluous adi-pose mattah ! " That's a plummy way of saying one's a little too fat!

Miss J. But tell me all about it, my Lord, while I tidy up the flowers; for the landlady has kindly allowed me to attend to the garden here.

Lord S. (*while going on with his ice*). Well, dear girl! as I was saying, it's such a splendacious spree! Tracts and gruel! if my *tyrannizer* hasn't arrived.

Miss J. Your *what*, my Lord?

Lord S. My "tyrannizer," that's what we call our Governors at Eton. And, d'ye see, my ancient Stick-in-the-mud thinks I'm working my fat down with a pedestrian tour through the Black Forest. But walking's an awful bore,—unless, indeed, its walking into an icedpudding.

Miss J. The little prize-pig! (*she is about to take the watering-pot to the pump against the stable wall at* R., *when* Lord S. *rises with an effort, and goes and detains her.*)

Lord S. Oh, Miss Jetsam! I couldn't think of allowing you. (*aside*) What a nuisance it is to have to move on a full stomach! (*takes the can from her, and goes and hangs it over the spout of the pump. He then begins working away at the handle but without raising any water at first.*) Well, I was (*gasping*) telling you, Miss Jetsam (*gasping again*) about my old Governor (*pausing for breath*). (Was there ever such a pump?) (*keeps on pumping and puffing as he talks*) You must know, then, I was looking over the " Travellers' Book " just now. (There goes one of my brace buttons, by Gum!) when whose name should I spot but that of my guardian. (*If this isn't a breather, may I be blowed!*) So I said to myself, Silverspoon, my boy, it's a case of (*exultingly as he sees the water beginning to flow*) up the spout at last!

MISS J. (*as* LORD S. *brings the can towards her*). Thank you, my Lord! A thousand thanks! But how it has made you pant, to be sure.

LORD S. (*nearly out of breath*). And now, I suppo e, I may be allowed— as a sweetener for my pains—to stop and do a little raking with you? (*puts his arm round her waist.*)

MISS J. (*pushing his arm away*). My Lord! Excuse me, but, if Lord Silverspoon were anything of a gardener, he would know how to train his tu-lips better than he seems to do.

LORD S. To my mind, Miss Jetsam, there is no prettier flower than the blush-rose; but much as I love to see it spring up in the virgin soil, I do not care to *raise* it. So pardon me, I beg (*lifts his hat respectfully and returns to his seat* L.).

MISS J. (*aside*). Well! he may be a little thoughtless coxcomb, but at least he's a little English gentleman.

LORD S. (*sitting down at table* L.) So now, as we're good friends again, Miss Jetsam, I suppose you'll have no objection, while you're attending to the weeds there, to my going in for a weed myself?

MISS J. Certainly not! if you wish it, my Lord. (*Then as she sees him about to light a cigarette*) But you never mean to say you smoke— at your tender age!

LORD S. (*indignantly*). What d'ye mean by *my* tender age? (*rises and brings her down* C., *and thrusts his face close up to hers, as he raises himself on tiptoe, and endeavours, while smoking, to curl the little bit of down on his upper lip.*) Have you observed my mustachios, Miss? (*comes down*).

MISS J. (*laughing*). No, my Lord! I don't happen to wear magnifying glasses. And, so far as I can see, it's more of the hair-presumptive than the hair-apparent.

LORD S. (*turning away in a huff*). Enough! I don't want to speak to you any more, Miss! (*goes and throws himself into his chair—and kicks over the opposite one in his temper.*)

MISS J. (*aside*). It's a shame to tease the poor little spoilt child of fortune.

LORD S. (*starting from his seat, and shaking himself*). Come! it's no use sulking! (*then going towards her, he says, tenderly*) There, let *me* water the flowers.

*They proceed to do the gardening together—*MISS JETSAM *arranging one part of the flower-bed while* LORD S. *waters the plants in another.*

LORD S. You expect your people up here shortly.

MISS J. Yes, my Lord! I was sent on with the maid from Geneva to bespeak apartments for them. Mr. Chirpey is bent upon trying to ascend Mont Blanc. Your Lordship, I think, said that *you* meant to go up?

LORD S. Ye-es! every fellah does Mont Blanc now; and what every fellah does, of course another fellah is obliged to do. For my part I wish Mont Blanc was at the bottom of the sea. But I'm bound to go up, because I'm so fat that I must get pulled down.

MISS J. Your Lordship means to join the party to-morrow?

LORD S. Ye-es, my fairy! If I can only steer clear of my *tyranniser*. But, oh crumbs! (*drops the watering-pot*) talk of the old gentleman, and there he is in the "*salle à manger*" by the sacred Jingo! (*runs and hides behind Miss J.*) Spread out your hind-feathers like a peacock, my guardian angel. So! But Jupiter Toe-nails! there's old Stars-

and-Garters at the window (*the* EARL OF O. *looks out into the garden*). Now go sidling along towards the doorway yonder, like the Ghost in the "Corsican Brothers" (*twisting her round a little*). That's it! Go along! And now (*melodramatically, as he reaches the hotel-door, and carries her in his arms into the hall*) my chey-ild! my chey-ild! we're saved! *Exeunt* R. 2 E.

Enter FRITZ C.

FRITZ (*going to the coffee-table at* L). So-oh! the young Milor has not his pudding eaten (*finishes it himself*). Smacks vare delica-at! Young Milor has blenty golt in de bocket—buy blenty zoabs—lofe de "Browns Vindsors." Shermans and Frenchmans not yearn for zoabs; for de sake dat Shermans and Frenchmans not so tirty than Englisher beobles. But I lofe de tirty beobles. Yah! give me mine "Browns Vindsors" and de tirty beobles. Vare fine bouquet! Vare goot market. (*Gate-bell rings without.*) Hah! de clock zounds one time more! De Golten Lion vags his dail for bleasure.

Enter MRS. CHIRPEY, L. 1 E.

MRS. C. (*as entering and speaking off.*) Now, Mr. Chirpey, when you've quite done chucking those ugly Swiss girls under the chin, perhaps you'll attend to me.

Enter PORTER, *wheeling on truck laden with luggage and a large Sitzbath on top,* L. 1 E.

CHIRPEY (*without*). Hoi! Hoi!

Enter CHIRPEY *running* L. 1 E.

MR. CHIRPEY *is dressed in a long grey Ulster coat. He carries an Alpenstock in one hand, and a* "MURRAY'S GUIDE" *in the other, and has several carved Swiss toys stuffed into his pockets. Over his shoulders is slung the usual* RIESE-TASCHE, *as well as field glass borne by tourists.*

CHIRPEY (*to* PORTER, *who is wheeling luggage towards door at* R. 2 E). Hoi! hoi! (*to* MRS. C.) What's the German for "hoi!" my dear? (*to* PORTER) Stop, you mutton-headed mountaineer! Where are you going to with those things, before I've counted 'em? Let me see! fifteen sticks! The fools here call all one's traps "sticks" (*proceeding to count boxes*). The ladies' trunks—five sticks! ladies' bonnet boxes—six more sticks! eleven sticks! Mr. Chirpey's portmanteau—twelve sticks! Mr. Chirpey himself—another stick! thirteen sticks! Mrs. Chirpey's sitz-bath—fourteen sticks! and partner of Mr. Chirpey's bosom (*putting his hand to his heart*) the last, and not the least, stick of all! (*to* PORTER) And now, cut *your* stick. *Exit* PORTER *with luggage,* R. 2 E.

FRITZ (*coming forward* L. *and bowing*). Velcome to de Herr Barone and his high-and-vellborn lady vife! Vat for schambers does the Herr Barone neet? two sleeb-schambers—hm?

MRS. C. (*at* R., *and in a whisper to* CHIRPEY). Tell the young man we want only *one* bedroom for ourselves, with *one large* bed in it.

CHIRPEY (*at* C.) A large bed! I should rather think we did!

MRS. C. Tell him, Mr. Chirpey, that a horrid little child's-crib for a bedstead wont suit *me*.

CHIRPEY. I should rather think it wouldn't! (*to* FRITZ) You hear what the lady says; and, if I might make a suggestion, I should prefer to sleep with the feather-bed *under* me, rather than *on* top. (*to himself*) For, as Mrs. Chirpey is a somewhat roomy party, it's apt to get disarranged in the course of the night.

Mrs. C. (*pettishly*). I never knew such a man as you are, Chirpey—standing there chattering to the waiter—and when you know I'm so poorly!

Fritz (*who is about to go off, but suddenly returns, and takes cake of soap out of his pocket, which he is about to offer to* Chirpey; *but, seeing him engaged with* Mrs. C., *shrugs his shoulders, and, having smelt it, puts it back, with a sigh, into his coat*). No! no! von oder time! I vill zoab him later.

Exit Fritz C., *taking off coffee-cup and gardening tools with him*.

Chirpey. Anything for peace and comfort, my dear. But why won't you take things as they are? Look at me; I'm fifty-five next birthday, and as lively as a two-year old.

Mrs. C. Ah! but if you only had my delicate nerves! Dr. Bogus, you know, said it was all my nerves.

Chirpey. Nerves! fiddlestrings! why can't you look on the bright side of things like me? Why will you always be scraping all the silver off the looking-glass? (*slapping her on the shoulder*). Come, pull yourself together, old girl! and put your best leg foremost.

Mrs. C. (*haughtily*). Mr. Chirpey! you ought to know, Sir, that both my legs are alike. If your constitution was only as shattered as mine, you'd be (*commencing to whimper*) low-spirited. Didn't Dr. Bogus tell me I should have been dead long ago if it hadn't been for my naturally-fine constitution?

Chirpey. Well, my dear, and haven't I done everything that a trueborn Briton could to uphold the glorious Constitution? Didn't I bring you all the way up the Rhine to drink the beastly waters that you *would* have it were the only things to give a stay to your stomach?

Mrs. C. (*pathetically*). Mr. Chirpey, Sir! How can you? and when you know I'm so poorly.

Chirpey. Didn't I, at Ems, stand calmly by—like a man—and see you take your fill of that disgusting sulphuretted stuff that smelt like gas-works and tasted like "Sour-Kraut?"

Mrs. C. Well! and I'm sure it did my liver a power of good.

Chirpey. Didn't I——

Miss Jetsam (*opening the French window of the "entresol" over the* Salle à Manger, *and putting her head out, with a hair brush in her hand—excitedly*). Oh, Mrs. Chirpey! I was coming down! I've just seen Florence out there (*pointing off* L.). Something's happened, I'm afraid! Yonder she comes, with half the town after her! Run, Mr. Chirpey! run, quick!

Chirpey (*hurrying off* L. 1 E.). I'm off like a two-year old.

Mrs. C. (*taking out her smelling salts*). Oh dear, oh dear! all my appalling presentiments are coming as true as those awful *horrorscopes* in Zadkiel's almanac! I knew that girl would break her neck with her horse-riding. I can see her now laid out a corpse at my feet.

(*Noise without.*)

Enter Miss Jetsam, L. U .E. *She runs up to* Mrs. Chirpey, *and, shaking her warmly by the hand, endeavours to console her*.

Oh, Miss Jetsam, my dear! support me. (Miss J. *leads her to table* R. *and* Mrs. C. *begins to take some homœopathic globules*.)

Florence (*without*). Be off with you! I'm not hurt!

Enter Florence, *in riding-habit, with hat and whip*, L. 1 E. *She is attended by* Chirpey, *and followed by a crowd of* Swiss Peasants *and* Villagers.

Florence (*brushing her habit with her handkerchief*). Haven't even "barked" myself (*kisses* CHIRPEY). Poor old Daddy! was he frightened then? (*to* CROWD) What are you staring at? Did you never see a person come a "cropper" before? (CHIRPEY *feels her arms as if to discover whether any bones are broken*) Pshaw, Dad! I'm as sound as a bell. But *do* send these yokels about their business, Daddy dear! (*laughing*) And here's the poor Mum! half-dead I declare!

CHIRPEY (*taking a handful of coppers out of his pocket, and throwing them off at* L. 1 E.). Go after that, you band of rapscallion republicans! *Exeunt* CROWD L. 1 E.

FLORENCE. And here's my darling Carry too! all of a tremble, like an Italian greyhound. (*to* CHIRPEY) I told you when we parted at Sallenches this morning I'd be here as soon as you were, Dad; and so I should too, if it hadn't been for that "weedy screw." I made him go, though, for once in his life. (Are you better, mother?) I gave him a "breather"—rattled him across the little bit of the valley, Carry, as if the hounds were before me. And when I'd made up my mind to come into the village with a dash, Daddy, why, may I never clear a "bullfinch" again, if the girths of the ramshackle old saddle didn't begin to loosen, and——

MRS. C. (*dolefully*). It's a mercy, girl, your mangled body wasn't brought to us on a shutter.

CHIRPEY. Ah! I thought something of this kind would happen, when you *would* have your riding-habit packed up with the rest of your traps.

FLORENCE. But then, Dad, you never told us you were coming up to such a "stiff country" as this.

MISS J. And may I be allowed to inquire, Mr. Chirpey, why you really *did* bring us up to these Alpine regions (*places chair for* CHIRPEY *opposite* MRS. C.).

CHIRPEY. Well, if you must know, Miss Jetsam, it is because I'm resolved not to remain a mere pigmy in the world; and determined to see how contemptibly small one's fellow-creatures appear when viewed from the summit of Mont Blanc (*sitting L. of table R.*).

FLORENCE. The idea, Dad, of you going to "do" Mont Blanc! A man of your years.

CHIRPEY. Just leave my years alone, will you! Yes, Miss; *I* mean to do Mont Blanc! (*The two girls talk together up* R.).

MRS. C. Well, Mr. Chirpey! you've insured your life—that's one comfort. (*Then taking him aside, and appealing to him in a pathetic tone.*) But have you no regard for your neck, rash man? would you fly in the face of Providence, and invalidate the policy?

CHIRPEY (*with a mock melodramatic air*). No matter, Madam, I've said it, and, may I become a potted shrimp, but I'll *do* it!

FLORENCE (*coming down behind chair and patting him on the back*) And I'll take short odds that the Governor goes in, and wins.

CHIRPEY. Aye, that I will, in a canter!

FLORENCE (*putting her arm round her father's neck, coaxingly*). And you'll take your darling Flo up with you—won't you, Daddy dear?

CHIRPEY (*pushing her from him good-humouredly*). Go along with you, you little humbug!

MRS. C. (*rising and going to* CHIRPEY). Isn't it enough to risk your own life, Mr. Chirpey, without worrying me into an early grave by teaching your child to risk *hers* too?

CHIRPEY (*rising and stamping his foot indignantly*). And isn't it enough, Madam, for me to have left my business in Simmary Axe—my superior bloater paste and piccalilli—my real Indian curry-powder and cayenne—without being treated to such connubial pepper as this?

MRS. C. You ought to be ashamed of yourself, Mr. Chirpey. But, as you're all going, I won't be left here alone, to suffer a martyrdom of suspense; so, if you have to bring me down in my coffin, *I* shall go up with you !

CHIRPEY (*slapping her on the shoulder*). Bravo, old gal! There's life in the old 'oss yet. But mind you! there's to be no breaking down—and no shirking—fair heel and toe, old lady! You can't be wheeled up in a Bath-chair. So come along ! we'll go and arrange about the ascent. The Porter told me there's a party going up to-morrow. (*Going up with* MRS. C., *arm-in-arm, towards hotel-door*). And I shouldn't wonder, my dear, but that the bracing mountain air will do you a power of good (*imitating her*) especially as, you know, you're so poorly!

Exeunt MR. *and* MRS. CHIRPEY, R. U. E.

FLORENCE. Come along, Carry ; we'll back ourselves for a place ; though I'm afraid poor dear Mama will want to "lay on the field."

Exeunt FLORENCE *and* MISS JETSAM, R. C. D.

BAND *plays without.*

Enter GUESTS *from* C. *They are seen to rise from the table in the* SALLE À MANGER, *and to take their hats, &c., from off the stand in the room, as if the* TABLE D'HÔTE *was just finished. Some go off* L. 1 E., *either arm in arm, or else gesticulating to each other as if in earnest conversation, while others stay and seat themselves at the marble coffee-tables in the garden.*

WAITERS *come out and serve the latter with coffee, "petits verres," and cigars, and* SWISS PEASANTS *come on at* L. 1 E., *and offer toys, &c., to them.*

Enter PROFESSOR WINDBEUTEL *and* CAPITAINE ACHILLE FORTINBRAS *at* C. *They stand for a while on the other side of the open French window, bowing and scraping, as to which shall enter first.*

CAPTAIN F. Mille Pardons! aftare you! Permit me! No, I can't not (*drawing back*).

PROFR. W. (*apologetically*). I beg Herr Capitaine! (*entering*) Ach-a ! Ach-a ! Ach-a ! Ach !

CAPTAIN F. (*as he follows the* PROFESSOR). Non! non ! non ! 'Tisn't not posseeble ! "*Esprit*" mus' all-days go before coura-age !

PROFESSOR W. Not so, mine Herr Capitaine ! De ponderoseetay of de knowledge-outseeking-and-in-taking zoul too colossa-al is to make to himself de impertinentishkite bevore de feet-steps of great-hearted unfearingness to tread.

CAPTAIN F. You are vare mosh amiable ! I have ze honnore to shake my hand at you (*extending his hand to the* PROFESSOR).

PROFESSOR W. I also de proudness have my gombliment to make. I take mine *head* off to you (*raising his hat and shaking the* CAPTAIN *by the hand, whereupon they proceed to embrace*).

CAPTAIN F. (*aside, over the* PROFESSOR'S *shoulder*). Hein ! ze stoopeed peeg !

PROFESSOR W. (*aside, over the* CAPTAIN'S *shoulder*). Pfui ! de sheep's-head ! (*They separate from each other's arms.*)

They retire up R., *and continue gesticulating and fraternizing at table.*

Exeunt several of the GUESTS, L. 1 E. *and* L. U. E.

Enter CHIRPEY C. *in Tourist's suit, with long roll of paper concealed under his coat.*

CHIRPEY. Here Waiter ! Kellner ! a glass of brandy ! (*making a wry face*) Augh ! people little know what's going on underneath my waistcoat. I've just had a dish of ca'ves' flesh and pickled plums, which I mistook for the pickled walnuts I've been craving for ever since I left my native Simmary Axe; and hang me! if I wa*n't fool enough to swallow one of the beastly lumps of blacking when (*shuddering*) oh, lor'! oh, lor'! where *is* this glass of *eau de vie?* (*sits at table at* R.).

Enter FRITZ C. *with a small glass of Cognac on tray.*

FRITZ (*after having placed the brandy on one of the small tables, and then taken out a cake of soap, but which, on observing* CHIRPEY's *condition previous to swallowing the liquor, he replaces in his pocket*). No! no! von oder time. He look too vhite now to need zoab.

Exit FRITZ, R., *and some more of the* GUESTS, L. 1 E.

CHIRPEY (*smacking his lips after the goûts*). Ha-ah! Chirpey's himself again! Well (*rubbing his hands*), I've settled the preliminaries for the ascent. We're off to-morrow at cock-crow.

Exeunt the remainder of the GUESTS—*some* R. U. E. *others* L. 1 E.

(*Observing the* PROFESSOR *and the* CAPTAIN *talking at* R.) Halloa! (*rises*) all the people gone but those two Leicester Square-like ragamuffins! I wonder whether they are to be some of our "*companions de voyage*"? I'll ask him (*going up to* PROFESSOR, *who advances to meet him*). You *comprenny* English, Mounseer? you talkee my (*pointing down his throat*) tongue?

PROFESSOR W. *Ja wohl!* I can de Englisher speech speak so well as I mine own Sherman speech speak can.

CHIRPEY (*aside*). Well! if you're no greater dab at it, old buffer, than that, I can't say much for your proficiency. But, no matter! I'll tackle him in my own fashion. Look here, old cockalorum.

PROFESSOR W. Vas ist gockaloroom?

CHIRPEY. Why, cockalorum! Are you going to mount (*doing the pantomime for mounting up stairs*) up (*pointing to the "flies"*) there (*pointing off into distance*) to-morrow? (*pausing and scratching his head*) How the deuce is one to express to-morrow in pantomine?

PROFESSOR W. Yes, vell! I go next morning de vonder-peautiful greatness of Natoor to study. I go mine leedle mite to de vidout-measure-great riches of de Pheelosophie to give. I take vit me (*producing pocket-case of philosophical instruments*) mine baro-mater, mine dermo mater, and mine mecrosco-ope. Lif you vell!

Exit PROFESSOR WINDBEUTEL, L. 1 E.

CHIRPEY. Well, it strikes me that not-particularly-lively party isn't likely to break down in the ascent for want of staying power; for, goodness knows, *he's* long-winded enough (*crosses to* L.).

CAPTAIN F. (*crossing to* R., *and advancing to* CHIRPEY *as he raises his hat*). You have reason, Sare! He is von dreamare, and a vare sleepy dreamare, too. But in me myself you find anozare, and von mosh greatare object. Me I go mount ze mountain for von grande idday. I have him here (*tapping his forehead*). Von idday so imm*œ*nse he break my head. I go pa'nt on high von name famoose—for all ze vorlt to see him. I have ze name here (*tapping his bosom*) gr-r-raven an-del-leebly on zis heart! I pa'nt him en-norme (*spreading out his arms so wide that he nearly slaps* CHIRPEY *in the face*). It is ze name of ma naschione, so ravishing! (*kissing the tips of his fingers*) Ze France! (*folding his arms across his bosom and shaking his head*) Ze beautiful France! (*lifting up both his hands, and shaking them high above his head*) And here ze brosh (*producing large whitewasher's implement*) vis vat I shall pan't hare. (*then bowing with great respect to* CHIRPEY, *as he takes his hat off to him*) Sare! I have ze honare you to sallute. (*aside*) Ze old cow of a Jean Bull!

Exit CAPTAIN FORTINBRAS, R. U. E.

CHIRPEY (*amazed*). Well! that fellow with his hat in his hand has certainly got a tile off; and his friend's upper-story doesn't appear to be in a state of very sound repair either. (*looks round to assure himself that nobody's about, and then in a confidential tone, as he takes stage* L.) But I've not mentioned why *I'm* going up Mont Blanc to a soul (*pulls chair forward, and sits astride of it, with the back facing the audience, and puts his fingers to his lips and whispers*). Kept it a profound secret even from the partner of my four-poster (*takes roll of canvas from under his coat, places it across his knees so that the bottom of the roll is uppermost, and then, unrolling a portion of it, contemplates it admiringly*). Beautiful! But wouldn't have it seen till the proper time.

Enter HON. MR. CENTLIVRE, L. 1 E., *with valise in his hand.* CHIRPEY, *on seeing him, leans suddenly over the back of his chair, so as to conceal the roll before him, and begins whistling as with an unconcerned air.*

Exit CENTLIVRE R. 2 E. *into* "BUREAU" *at* L., *where he is seen to converse with the lady in the office.*

He didn't see me! "CHIRPEY," said I to myself when the brilliant idea first flashed upon me, "you're the proud inventor of a delicious new condiment—christened—after a long series of sleepless nights—'THE SHAH'S DELIGHT, *or, Persian Persuasive Pickle.*' But," said I, "nothing's done now-a-days, Chirpey, without advertising and puffing; and the secret of advertising consists in puffing away till you're read in every part." "Then," said I to myself once more, "Chirpey! you be off at once and put up a poster of your delicious 'Persuasive Pickles' on the summit of Mont Blanc so that the eyes of Europe may be upon it." "*I will!*" I cried. "The world owes me a debt of gratitude for the delectable discovery, and so—there's my little bill!" (*he lets the end of the roller drop down over the chair-back, so as to expose to the audience a large coloured placard, representing the* SHAH OF PERSIA *seated cross-legged devouring pickles, and with the words* "THE SHAH'S DELIGHT" *printed in large letters underneath it. This he leaves hanging over the top of the chair, and, rising from his seat, comes down to the front, and admires it as he rubs his hands exultingly*) There's high art for you! Idea, too, as novel as the design, and as brilliant as the colours. The German's going up Mont Blanc (*imitating the* PROFESSOR) "to study Natoor!" Chirpey's going up (*winks*) to study his own interest! The Frenchman's going up (*imitating the* CAPTAIN) "for ze glory of ze France." Chirpey, like a true-born Englishman, is going up (*plunging his hands into his breeches pockets and playing with his money*) for the sake of the shop! For what's philosophy or patriotism to Chirpey, in comparison with his own business? (*points triumphantly to the posting-bill*) Why it's all pickles!

MRS. C. *appears on balcony* C.

MRS. C. (*in a loud and angry voice*). Wherever have you got to, Mr. Chirpey? *Exit* MRS. C.

CHIRPEY (*in a bland tone, as he discovers* MRS. C). Coming, my heart's comforter! (*then dolefully, as he hides the roll behind him*) Now I shall have it hot and sharp as my best Chili vinegar. Coming, my sweetest!

Exit CHIRPEY, *holding the pickle bill spread out behind him*, R. U. E.

Enter the HON. PERCY CENTLIVRE *with a book in his hand* R. 2 E. *He crosses over to one of the marble tables at* L, *and seats himself with his back towards* R.

CENTLIVRE (*opening the volume, as he lays it before him on the table* L, *and then taking out his note-book*). Can't get any tidings of the puss in boots, nor yet of the old cat in mittens, her mother. Surely one can't have come all this way on a fool's errand? Haven't been wasting my time though, while coming up here—read the whole of Sheridan's speeches (*taking up book*) through in the car from Geneva to Sallenches. And, by the bye, that reminds me—there's a passage here (*taking up volume*) I just wanted to make a note of (*sits at table L, proceeds to light a cigar and make an extract from the volume into his memorandum-book, and continues writing*).

Enter HAROLD MAJORIBANKS, L. 1 E. *and crossing to* R. *table.* HAROLD *is habited as for a walking tour. He wears white flannel trousers and shirt, no waistcoat, light tweed jacket, straw hat, and thick lace-up boots, which are covered with dust. On his back he carries a knapsack, with a pair of canvass shoes strapped on top.*

HAROLD M. Ha-ah! here's dear old Chamouni again! That's all right (*crosses, places his knapsack on one of the small tables* R., *and throws himself, as if tired, at full length on the rustic bench at* R.). (*Takes off his straw hat and wipes his forehead as he looks at his watch*). Come! I did that last bit from the valley of Châtelas in little better than two hours (*undoes his knapsack*). Let me see now! where's my map? No! that's the carte-de-visite of FLORENCE, which I bought at the Baden-Baden photographer's. Bless her pretty face! (*kisses the portrait*) Ah! here's the plan of the country (*takes out map and spreads it open upon his knees*); and now which way did I come? But first for a smoke (*takes out cigarcase and lights a cigar with the last match in the match-holder*). Haven't done a cloud since my last halt (*then proceeds to trace his route with his forefinger on the map*). Yes, that's it! past Bonneville and Cluses; then on to St. Martin and St. Gervais; and then—hang these Swiss things! can't get 'em to draw; and, confound it! there are no more matches. I'll ask the industrious stranger yonder for a light. (*rises, and goes over to* CENTLIVRE) Would you allow me to intrude upon your studies so far as to beg a light from your cigar?

CENTLIVRE. Oh, with pleasure! (*he turns round,* HAROLD *proceeds to take a light from* CENT'*s cigar, and, as he does so, they start and recognise one another.*)

HAROLD M. (*recognising* CENTLIVRE). Why, Percy! what on earth brings *you* up to Mont Blanc? I thought you cared more about reading up classics than climbing up mountains.

CENTLIVRE. And *I* fancied, Harold, you'd had your fill of such breakneck adventures and were off on a walking tour.

HAROLD M. Excuse me, old boy! I've been on my legs long enough to day; so with your permission I'll take it easy. (*goes back to bench at* R. *and lolls at one end of it.*) You told me you were going to remain at Baden-Baden, studying International law, grinding the dry bones of Vatel, Puffendorf, and Grotius into your brains—in fact, cramming away like a Strasbourg goose.

CENTLIVRE. (*crossing to bench, and sitting astride at the opposite end of it*). And you gave me to understand you were going to bring your weight down by doing five and twenty miles a day over the Hartz.

HAROLD M. Tell me what's up?

CENTLIVRE (*somewhat huffy*). What's up with yourself?

HAROLD M. Here, Waiter, bring me a "*petit verre!*" Oh! I'll make a clean breast of it, if you will.

CENTLIVRE. H—m! Well, *you* lead off!

HAROLD M. And you'll follow suit, mind! (CENTLIVRE *nods and smiles.* HAROLD *then leans over towards him, pokes him in the ribs with his stick, and says laughingly in a half-whisper*) I'm here after a devilish fine girl.

CENTLIVRE. No, you don't say so! (*laughing and poking* HAROLD *in the ribs with the edge of the book he has in his hand*) And I'm playing the same little game.

HAROLD M. Oh! naughty Mr. *Saint*-livre—and at your time of life!

CENTLIVRE. What d'ye mean by my time of life? Come, I'm so *very* much your senior.

HAROLD M. But, tell me, what's *your* girl like? *Mine's* an angel in the prettiest "*bottines*" in the world (*kissing his finger tips*).

CENTLIVRE (*clasping his hands*). And mine's a Venus, with the loveliest head of golden hair in the universe.

HAROLD M. (*amazed*). H—m! mine's got golden hair! and such eyes—the softest hazel!

CENTLIVRE (*puzzled*). H—m! *My* girl's eyes are hazel too.

HAROLD M. I say, old fellow! *your* girl's never the one we used to meet at the *table d'hôte* at Baden-Baden?

CENTLIVRE. You've hit the right nail on the head, by George!

HAROLD M. The deuce I have! I never dreamt you were spooney upon *her*. I thought *I'd* got that lovely creature all to myself.

CENTLIVRE. And *I* fancied *I* was managing the matter most dexterously, by keeping you so nicely in the dark. But what's to be done?

HAROLD M. (*jumping up from his seat*). All I can see is: one of us must clear out.

CENTLIVRE. That's it! you go! (*they rise, and cross* C.)

HAROLD M. Go yourself, and see how you like it. (*gravely*) I should tell you, Centlivre, this is a very *se-*rious matter to me. *I'm* not going to trifle with the girl—*I* mean to marry her.

CENTLIVRE. And *I*, Majoribanks, have made up my mind to propose at the first opportunity.

HAROLD M. You! (*then as if remonstrating with him*). I say, Centlivre, a man in your position! at your time of life, too! and the scion of a noble house! to think of linking yourself with an oil and Italian warehouse!

CENTLIVRE. And doesn't it strike you, Majoribanks, that the son of one of the most fashionable physicians in England might do better than mix up medicine with pickles and preserves?

HAROLD M. Well! we can't both have the girl, that's clear!

CENTLIVRE. Who's to decide which shall?—that's the point.

HAROLD M. Why, let the girl herself be umpire.

CENTLIVRE. That's it! You do all you can to ingratiate yourself with the lady.

HAROLD M. And you make love to her as passionately as you please.

CENTLIVRE. We'll each wage war in our own fashion. I shall bring my diplomatic training into play.

HAROLD M. And I shall break a lance with you like a knight-errant. If *you* are triumphant, Percy, I shall make you a very low bow and retire.

CENTLIVRE. And if *you* carry her off, Harold, I promise you I won't bear you any ill-will, old boy.

HAROLD M. We'll continue the same good friends. And, what's more, the loser shall be the "best man" at the wedding of the winner.

CENTLIVRE. Agreed!

HAROLD M. It's to be a friendly struggle.

CENTLIVRE. Yes, a chivalrous contest! (*both at* R.) Come! the hand before the battle (*extending his palm to him*).

HAROLD M. (*grasping it and shaking it cordially*). Yes! and remember! the hand *after* it too.

Enter FLORENCE *and* MRS. C. *from open French window* C. *They come down* L. FLORENCE *has changed her dress. She wears a fashionable costume, and carries in her hand a small flower-basket, in which is placed her handkerchief.*

(*Putting his hand over* CENTLIVRE'S *mouth, and in a whisper as he nudges him*). Sh—sh, man! here's the girl herself!

FLORENCE. And now to see what Miss Jetsam's garden's like. (*As she comes down to the front, she drops her handkerchief out of the basket, whereupon* CENTLIVRE *and* HAROLD *both rush different ways round the flower-bed at* C *to pick it up.* CENTLIVRE *gets to it first and returns exultingly with it to* FLORENCE, *whilst* HAROLD M. *goes through the pantomime of punching his own head.*)

CENTLIVRE (*bowing as he takes off his hat, and presents handkerchief*). This, I think, belongs to you, Madam?

HAROLD M. (*shrugging his shoulders, throwing up his hands, and going back to* R.). There's a splendid start he's got! and here am I left at the post.

(*Lights gradually lowered.*)

CENTLIVRE (*embarrassed*). I'm charmed—a—a—to have the good fortune—a—a—of restoring the property—a—a—to its fair owner. (*aside*) Hang it! what *was* that Sir Walter Raleigh said to Queen Elizabeth?

HAROLD M. Don't ask me!

FLORENCE (*as she returns* CENTLIVRE'S *bow*). Oh, thanks! (*recognising him*). Mr. Centlivre, if I'm not mistaken?

MRS. C. (*aside, as she plucks* FLORENCE *by the skirt*). Florence dear, who is the young man? Why don't you introduce me?

FLORENCE (*introducing* MRS. C.). Don't you remember, Mama?—the gentleman who was so polite to us at Baden-Baden.

MRS. C. *curtseys and* MR. CENTLIVRE *bows.*

HAROLD M. (*aside*). As I'm left out in the cold here, I'll do a cough (*coughs sepulchrally*).

FLORENCE (*starting*). Gracious! whatever is that? (HAROLD M. *comes forward, still pretending to cough*) It's your friend, Mr. Majoribanks! Why didn't you tell us he was here? (*bowing to* HAROLD M.) So delighted! And are *you* up here with that dreadful cold upon you?

CENTLIVRE (*aside*). He never had it before. Getting up the girl's sympathy under false pretences. I'll be even with him. (*revengefully*) I'll put him off on the old lady. (*comes down* L.)

HAROLD M. It's extremely kind of Miss Florence! and the pity she has been so good as to express is the more delightful because, as the poet says, you know—Pity is akin to—

CENTLIVRE, *on purpose to drown the end of the sentence, throws over one of the coffee-tables at* L.

FLORENCE *and* MRS. C. *are startled by the noise.*

HAROLD M. Don't be alarmed. It's only Mr. Centlivre! (*witheringly*) And his nervousness invariably makes him awkward in the society of ladies.

CENTLIVRE (*at* L. C. *aside*). *Et tu Brute!*

FLORENCE. But, Mr. Majoribanks! I am sure, Mama—whom you recollect at Baden (*introducing him*)—would be only too glad to let you have some of her excellent remedies for chest-complaints.

CENTLIVRE (*aside, as he rushes forward*). Oh, beautiful! grand opportunity! for shutting him up with a confab with the old mother. (*runs round to* R., *and takes* HAROLD M. *by the arm to* MRS. C.) Yes, Madam!

Aст I.   MONT BLANC.   21

the poor young man has been ailing a long time here (*tapping his chest, while* HAROLD M. *kicks out at him behind*), and it would be the greatest possible charity if you would recommend him some of your invaluable recipes.

HAROLD M. (*aside*). Oh, you villain! you've caught me in my own trap.

MRS. C. (*to* HAROLD M.). I've suffered from all kinds of chest-complaints myself, my dear young man—dreadfully in my time. Bronchitis, pulmonia, asthma, pleurisy, and, indeed, I don't know what. And, I'm sure, I shall only be too happy——But first let me ask you (*takes hold of him by the button*) have you ever tried "DR. DILLWATER'S BRONCHIAL BRANDY-BALLS?" (*leads him over to* L., *where she continues talking to him impressively, while he keeps fidgeting as he watches* CENTLIVRE's *attention to* FLORENCE.)

CENTLIVRE. I think I heard Miss Florence say she had come to look at the flowers. (*going to flower-bed*). Will she permit me to gather some for her? There's a lovely tea-rose there! allow me to pluck it.

FLORENCE. Thanks! I can't bear the sallow-looking things. The tea-rose always seems to me as if it were the jaundiced Old Maid of the Garden; and I'm sure she must think all the pretty blush-roses are painted. But here's a splendid damask-rose I must have (*plucks it, crosses to* C., *and lets it fall as she gives a slight scream*).

CENTLIVRE (*at* R., *compassionately*). Has the presumptuous thorn dared to wound those pretty little fingers?

FLORENCE (R.C.). Very feeble, Mr. Centlivre! you ought rather to have inquired, in sporting phraseology, if "the favourite had been scratched" (*puts the finger in her mouth, and sucks it as she talks*). Have you such a thing as a piece of sticking-plaister?

CENTLIVRE (*feeling confusedly in his pockets*). Sticking-plaister! I really don't think! But I'll run immediately! (*about to run off, but returns* C.)

HAROLD M. (*bursting from* MRS. C. *and rushing towards* FLORENCE). Court-plaister I have, and at Miss Florence's service! (*takes out pocketbook with scissors and plaister in it*) Allow me! (*takes hold of her hand*) I'll be as tender as possible, I can assure you.

CENTLIVRE (*aside*.) Deuce take his court-plaister! It'll stick to me for life. I'll never travel again without an acre of it in my pocket.

FLORENCE. You're awfully kind! But have you any pink?

HAROLD M. Certainly! But I'm afraid the most delicate pink would never match a hand that is as fair and sweet as Chamouni honey.

CENTLIVRE (*aside*). The scoundrel's squeezing it.

HAROLD M. (*putting the plaister on*). There! I think you will find *that* will effectually heal the wound.

FLORENCE (*withdrawing her hand, which he tries to keep locked in his*). That will do, thank you! Hands down is the proper way to be winning.

HAROLD M. I beg your pardon, don't you think it requires just a *leetle* more pressure? (FLORENCE *shakes her head and laughs.*)

MRS. C. (*at* R.) Are you gentlemen going to join the party for the ascent to-morrow?

HAROLD M. *and* CENTLIVRE *look at each other embarrassed.*

HAROLD M. Are you going, Centlivre?

CENTLIVRE. No! (*aside*) Florence is not going of course; so I'll just put Mr. Harold in for it. (*to* FLORENCE) I don't care about it myself; but my friend Majoribanks here means to venture (*with mock pathos*). For, rash young man! he *will* insist on braving the dangers and leaving his old friend behind—with you — anxiously waiting for the news as to whether or not he has—(*spitefully*) broken his neck!

HAROLD M. (*to* CENTLIVRE). You impudent wretch!
FLORENCE. I beg your pardon, Mr. Centlivre! In that case you will be left behind with the ruck—for this filly is going to start.
HAROLD M.
 and   } You, Miss Florence!
CENTLIVRE.
HAROLD M. *rubs his hands, and* CENTLIVRE *stamps his foot.*
CENTLIVRE. Oh, then, I shall certainly enter for the race.
MRS. C. Yes! and I am sure you gentlemen will be gratified to hear that *I* mean to make one of the party as well.
HAROLD M.
 and   } You, Mrs. Chirpey!
CENTLIVRE.
HAROLD M. (*aside*). Now it's my turn to handicap him with the weight of the old lady (*crosses to* MRS. C., *and leads her to* CENTLIVRE). Then allow me, Madam, to place you under the care of one of the most sure-footed creatures in the world, with a considerable length of *years* over his head, and one who would be only too glad (rather than you should fail in the attempt) to place you on his back, and carry you to the summit. As for myself (*bowing*) I shall be most happy to take care of your daughter.
CENTLIVRE (*aside*). You bare-faced impostor!

Lights in front turned slightly down. Table d'hôte room and hall of hotel lighted up.

MRS. C. (*going up* R.) Dear me! how the evenings begin to draw in, and we're not half through the autumn yet. (*shuddering*) It's growing quite chilly, I declare! Come, Florence! let's get indoors. I daren't trust myself to the night air.
FLORENCE. Stay, Mama! what's all this! (*turning round.*)

Enter GUIDES *from* L. 1 E, *with lanterns*—M. *and* MR. LAVIGNE *follow with* FRITZ *and* WAITERS *bringing out hampers, &c. Other hotel* ATTENDANTS *also come on and light the coloured lamps arranged round the garden-beds and over the table-d'hôte-room windows. Footlights down.*

M. LAVIGNE. Now let all those who intend making the ascent to-morrow morning assemble. (*to* WAITERS) Run you Fritz and Alphonse and muster the party here, so that they may be introduced to the Guides.
Exit 2ND WAITER, L. U. E.
FRITZ (*calling off into hall as he stands on the doorsteps*). Numero Zwelf, Monsieur Sheerpie! Herr Professor! Monsieur le Capitaine! Monsieur le Docteur! Young Milor!—all of you, come!
HAROLD M. (*recognising* FRANÇOIS *and shaking hands with him at* L.). Ah, François! *we* needn't wait to be formally introduced.
FRANÇOIS. Eh, parbleu! Is it you, Monsieur? you have come back to us then this year also?
HAROLD M. So you've not forgotten me—eh?
FRANÇOIS (*turning to the* GUIDE *next him*). Are *we* likely to, Baptiste? Would any Chamouni Guide ever forget the brave young Englander who saved poor Pierre from the crevasse on the Grand Plateau last season?

All the GUIDES *gather round* HAROLD M. *and shake him cordially by the hand.*

HAROLD M. There, that'll do! I only did for one of you what any one of you would have done for me; so no more about it.

Act I.   MONT BLANC.   23

Enter Professor Windbeutel *and* Captain Fortinbras *with another* Guide, L. 1 E.

Professor W. We gome our gomblements to de to-morrow-up-mounting barties to make. (*bows to all present.*)

Captain F. Messieurs et Mesdames! (*taking off hat and making sweeping bow to all*) I have ze honnare! Permit me to vish all ze persones good fortune and good voyage.

Florence (*aside to* Harold M.) Come, Mr. Majoribanks! half-a-dozen of gloves those two dark outsiders never see the winning-post. (Harold M. *shakes his head, and laughs*)

Enter Lord Silverspoon *and* Miss Jetsam C., *each with a shawl upon the arm.*

Miss J. I've brought your shawls with me, Mrs. Chirpey, and Florence dear.

Miss Jetsam *is about to arrange shawl over* Mrs. C.'*s shoulders, at* R., *when*

Professor *and* Captain *rush up.*

Professor W. *and* } (*both rushing across to* R.) { Ach-a Ach-a Ach!
Captain F. } { No! no! no! I could not nevare!

They each take hold of one end of the shawl, and struggle as to which shall put it on—much to Mrs. C.'*s discomfiture. While this is going on, young* Lord S., *standing on tiptoe, proceeds to put the shawl he has brought on* Florence'*s shoulders at* R., *and is discovered in the act by* Centlivre, *who runs up to perform the same office.*

Lord S. Cousin Centlivre by Gum!

Centlivre (*taking* Lord S. *by the ear*). You young vagabond! Is this the Black Forest?

Lord S. (*breaking away from him, and putting himself on guard with his arm*). And is *this* cramming away at Baden-Baden like a Strasbourg goose? But I say Cent., (*whispers*) the Governor's here! Dont you peach on me, and I won't split on you.

Centlivre. The Governor here! Then I must study a little more diplomacy.

Enter Captain Broadside, Dr. Majoribanks, *and* Earl of Osborne, L. U. E.

Captain B. (*to* Dr. M. *and* Earl of O. *as he stands on the door-steps*). I tell you, gentlemen, seven francs for that last bottle of wine is down-right infernal imposition! and, damn me, if I don't write to "The Times" about it!   *Exit* Captain B. *at* R. C.

Earl of O. (*to* Dr. M. *as they come down together*). Yes, Doctor! I've gone carefully over the "Travellers' Book," and my son's name isn't among this week's arrivals.

Dr. M. Nor is my lad's name there, my—that is Mr. Osborne, and yet I know from the Police Authorities at Baden that Harold had his passport viséed for Charmouni.

Harold M. (*aside to* Centlivre) My Governor Cent., by all that's hard lines.

Centlivre. And mine by all that's equally unfortunate?

Lord S. And mine by all that's not-particularly-awfully jolly!

Centlivre. What's to be done?

Harold M. Let's change hats with the Guides! they'll do anything for me; and then we'll all right for to-morrow.

HAROLD M., CENTLIVRE, *and* LORD S. *hide among the* GUIDES *and take their hats in exchange for their own.*

M. LAVIGNE. Well, gentlemen! you're all assembled. François, the Head Guide here, will tell you what he will require of you in the morning.

MRS. C. But we're not all here yet, Landlord! Where's Mr. Chirpey?

MISS J. Ay, where *is* Mr. Chirpey?

FRITZ (*calling off*). Monsieur *Sheer*pie! Monsieur *Sheer*pie!

Enter CHIRPEY R. C., *with large Tyrolese belt in his hand, and* ALL VISITORS *from Hotel*).

CHIRPEY (*down C. and showing belt*). Look here, my dear! I think I've *rather* done it now. I bought this grand Tyrolese stomacher of that obliging young man (*pointing to* FRITZ). Been trying it on in front of the glass up-stairs; and allow me to assure you, Madam, that in my Alpine hat and check knickerbockers I look the very twin brother to the late lamented Mr. William Tell.

FRANCOIS (*coming forward*). *Eh bien*, gentlemen! The gun here will be fired in the morning half an hour before sunrise, and the Guides and mules, as well as the Porters and Volunteers, will then meet you.

M. LAVIGNE. Yes, gentlemen, and here are the hampers of good things which I have provided for you. You will find in them everything you require.

WAITERS *bring two of the hampers forward, and place them in front of* CHIRPEY. FRITZ *lifts the cover of one, and takes up successively some of the articles.*

FRITZ. Gold sheekens!
CHIRPEY. Not to be despised!
FRITZ. Roast feal and muddon!
CHIRPEY. Very tidy tackle!
FRITZ. Goffee!
CHIRPEY. Pretty bobbish!
FRITZ. Gans of gondensed millick!
CHIRPEY. The genuine article of course!
FRITZ. Dins of gravy zoup!
CHIRPEY. Very agreeable to the stomach!
FRITZ. And Gruyere sheese! (*handing a piece to* CHIRPEY.)

CHIRPEY (*smelling it and pushing it away disgustedly*). Not particularly agreeable to the nose. But halloa! what are we to do for swizzle? (*to* MRS. C.) What's the Swiss for swizzle, my dear?

FRITZ. Ah ze zweezale! here he is. (*pointing to other baskets*) Boutled beare! clar-ret! cognac! and shampan.

FRANCOIS. But the shampan is to be opened only when our talk is accomplished, and we have reached the summit at last.

CHIRPEY. No! no! I'm for summat at first. Here, open a bottle or two! I'll stand the shot. Bring out the glasses, and let's have bumpers all round. Chirpey will give you a toast! (WAITERS *proceed to hand glasses round, and to pour out champagne.*)

Enter TOWN CRIER, VILLAGERS, *and* PEASANTS, *some bearing lanterns, and others torches.*

TOWN CRIER (*as if reciting a speech, and emphasising words as marked*). The people of *Chamouni*—come to wish the ascending *party*——

CAPTAIN F. (*jumping forward*, R., *and bowing*). Good fort*une* and *bon voyage!*

CHIRPEY (*to* M. LAVIGNE). Give 'em some beer! (*mugs of beer handed round to* CROWD.) And now, are you all charged? (*jumps on chair and holds glass of champagne in air.*)
VILLAGERS, &c. Ay! Ay! (CROWD *cheers.*)
CHIRPEY. Order, there! order! Chair! chair! Well, then, here's may those who seek to magnify molehills into mountains always "get in a hole." (CROWD *cheers.*) But may *we*, who strive to reduce mountains to molehills, never fail to find friends, ready to lend us a hand, and give us a leg up—in our attempt at MONT BLANC.

GENERAL CHEERING *and* TABLEAU.

BAND *plays without.*

END OF ACT I.

ACT II.

ON THE GRANDS MULETS.

SCENE.—*The Cabin on the* "GRANDS MULETS"—*the* "MULETS" *being three large spines of rock standing amid glaciers. Only two of the spines are shown: one at* R. *and the other at* L. *side of stage—the Cabin itself being built up between the back and front* "*spurs*" *of the latter.*

The cloth at back represents MONT BLANC *in the extreme distance, with the* "ROCHERS ROUGES" *on one side of it, and the* "GRAND PLATEAU" *immediately below the* "CALOTTE" *or* "CAP." *Moon and stars* (*transparent*) *above* MONT BLANC, *but not lighted up at first—the time at the commencement of the Act being supposed to be just before sundown.*

Slightly in front of the cloth, and at L. C., *is the* 2ND MULET, *consisting of several* "*spurs*" *of rock made out in* "*profile.*" *In* 4th *Grooves,* L., *is a large row, on which is painted the 2nd Glacier, which projects nearly to the middle of the stage, and has a platform arranged behind it so as to admit of being ascended almost to the* "*flies.*" *On the* R. *side of the sloping platform the stage is cut away, in order that the ascent may be commenced from below. In* 1st *and* 3rd *Grooves are wings representing crags covered with snow and icicles.*

In a line with 3RD *and* 4TH GROOVES L. C., *the stage is cut away, so that the Entrances may be made from below.*

Then at R. *side—*3rd GROOVES—*is a profile reaching to* R. C. *of back spurs of* 1ST MULET. *Behind the first tall spur there is a flight of steps, admitting of its being ascended nearly to the top.*

The R. *wing—*2ND GROOVES—*shows the middle spur of the* 1ST MULET; *and at* 1ST GROOVES, *on same side, is another wing showing the front spur.*

Between the 1ST *and* 3RD GROOVES, R., *is the Cabin, built up and fitted with practicable door, two small windows, and chimney, the pipe from which passes through the second window, and with the* "*lean-to*" *roof heaped with snow, and having long icicles hanging from the eaves.*

In C., and in a line with 3rd E., *is an open trap covered with a large tissue-paper "mask," which is intended to represent a film of snow concealing a crevasse. Immediately at back of this are ledges of rocks, and in front of it are two large boulders, one of which is displaceable.*

The stage is covered with a cloth painted for broken ground strewn with boulders half-covered with snow; and there is a large boulder at R. I. E. *that admits of being used as a seat.*

On the rising of the curtain, GUIDES *are discovered in front at* L. C. *seated round a fire made on ground. Some are smoking, and others lying asleep on rugs. In front of cabin-windows are other* GUIDES *collecting in bottles water, which is seen to drip from thawing snow on the roof. From the pipe of the chimney through the farther window of the cabin smoke is seen to issue, and the windows have a strong red light shining through them, and tinting the snow without. The door is ajar, and the same lurid light shines through the opening. The stage is littered with hampers, ropes, axes, knapsacks, lanterns, and a long ladder with flat steps.*

Nearly at the top of the second back-spur of the 1ST MULET *is discovered* FRANÇOIS, *leaning over the edge of the rock, and peering through a telescope as if looking far below.*

Midway up this same spur is also discovered HAROLD MAJORIBANKS *standing with a cow-herd's horn in his hand, and leaning on his bâton, while he looks up towards* FRANÇOIS *as if intent upon learning what he sees.*

HAROLD M. What news, François?

FRANÇOIS. I see the people at Chamouni out in the market-place. They look no bigger than a swarm of ants on a mole-hill.

HAROLD M. They *must* have spotted us by this time.

FRANÇOIS. They have! There goes the tiny speck of a flag fluttering up the church-steeple.

HAROLD M. It's signal No. 1, that they've seen us. Keep a sharp look out now, François, for the firing of the gun.

FRANÇOIS (*starting*). Ha! there's the flash! I saw it—like the striking of a match in the dark (*getting up, and putting his finger to his wrist*). We shall hear the boom of it borne upon the wind before the pulse beats thirty.

HAROLD M. Silence! (*Some of the* GUIDES *rise and listen attentively. After a few seconds a muffled sound is heard without.*) Hark how it comes!—no louder than the drone of a bee. Let's answer them (*ties his red handkerchief to the end of his bâton, and hands it up to* FRANÇOIS, *who plants it atop of the spur*). And now to wake up the echoes and the sleepers (*blows horn*).

Those GUIDES *who have been asleep jump up, and commence unpacking hampers and putting out provisions for dinner. Whilst this is going on* HAROLD M. *and* FRANÇOIS *come down.*

FRANÇOIS (*at* C.). We shall have a fine night, Sir, for the ascent (*to* SECOND GUIDE)—shan't we, Baptiste? (*then pointing off to distance*) Mont Blanc, you see, is smoking his cigar.

HAROLD M. (*going to back of fire* L. C.). Ay! the evening mists begin to curl about the old fellow's white night-cap. It's a fair weather-sign, I know.

FRANÇOIS. But, to make sure, let you and I, Baptiste, go and sound the state of the ice (*pointing up*) upon the "*Montets*" yonder.

HAROLD M. You Guides are as wide-awake and watchful as marmots in the summer (*going up*). Come! I'll plod part of the way with you (*begins to descend the trap* L. C. *with the two* GUIDES, *and when half way halts*). But do you, François, before we leave, call the drowsy herd up with one of your rousing "*Ranz des Vaches.*" (FRANÇOIS *blows the Swiss call on his horn, and exit with* HAROLD M. *and* 2ND GUIDE *by trap* L.C.)

CHIRPEY (*with his eyes scarcely open, putting his head out of hut-window*) Police! move that brass band on to the next street (*opening his eyes*). Where am I? Halloa! it's been snowing.

Enter CHIRPEY *from cabin* R. *He wears a blue blouse, with a large Tyrolese belt round it, check knickerbockers, leather leggings tied with scarlet garters, a black-worsted "templar" head-piece, with Alpine hat, and green veil rolled round the brim; and he has large fur-gloves, without fingers, slung round his neck by a string.*

CHIRPEY (*with his hands in his gloves, and rubbing his eyes with the back of them*). Well! I never before had the miserable satisfaction of enjoying forty winks on the shelf of a refrigerator (*sniffs, rubs his nose with his fur-gloves, gets the hairs up his nostrils, and then pauses as if about to sneeze and could'nt*). How the hairs tickle! but there's no getting at one's pockets in these (*showing gloves*) "small sevens" (*groans as he attempts unguardedly to lift his legs*). O-o-oh! all the hinges of my body want oiling. My pulse is beating away as fast as an undertaker's hammer, and I've got a singing in my head for all the world as if my skull was a sea-shell. I feel as if I'd crammed six months at the treadmill into half-a-day's work (*turning to the* GUIDES, *who have just finished spreading the provisions on the ground*). Here's the cold dinner all getting colder. But I'll have 'em out of that (*begins making snow-balls from front and side of cabin*). Come out, you Rip Van Winkles! (*throws snow-balls into the cabin window; whereupon expostulating cries and angry oaths are heard within. Hides himself* R. 3 E.)

Enter CAPTAIN BROADSIDE, *from cabin* R.—*limping hurriedly.*

CAPTAIN B. *wears a pea-jacket, sou'-wester, and tarpaulin leggings. The* PROFESSOR *is dressed in his ordinary costume, but with the legs of his trousers tucked into the top of his short Wellington boots. Crossed over his bosom, and wrapped round his waist, in true German fashion, he wears a shepherd's-plaid shawl, and has a Panama straw hat on his head, with the brim bent down over his ears, and secured by a red cotton-handkerchief passed over the crown, and tied under the chin. He has also a pair of blue snow-spectacles, and a green veil falling down over the back of his neck.*

CAPTAIN FORTINBRAS *is completely enveloped in a Bernouse cloak, with the jelly-bag-like hood turned up over his head, and has likewise large blue spectacles protecting his eyes.*

CAPTAIN B. Come, avast there! firing chilled shot. Mast-head me! but that cabin's as close as the hold of a slave ship. May I be clapped into irons if I don't write to the "TIMES" about it! (*groaning*) Augh! catch me coming aloft again! My body's as sore as if I'd just had six dozen seized up to the gratings! (*goes to back of fire.*)

Enter PROFESSOR W. *from cabin* R.

PROFESSOR W. (*rubbing his back as he comes hobbling forward*). Ach-a! ach-a! ach-a! ach! De rheumateesmoose is nudding to it. (*goes up* C.)

Enter CAPTAIN F. *from cabin* R.

CAPTAIN F. (*who has gone limping over to* L. *to hunt for his pot of paint among the soup-cans, but starts up suddenly, clutching his loins, as if seised with a violent spasm*). Oh, dee-able! now I catch him!

PROFESSOR W. (*in a state of philosophic rapture at the sight of the view*). How golossa-al ist de Natoor! I durn round mineself and feel (*is about to wave his arms, and take a sweeping survey of the landscape, but is suddenly stopped by a "crick" in the back*). Autch!

CAPTAIN F. (*still searching, with one hand to his back, and the other routing among the soup-cans*). Vare is ma pant? I have ze brosse here. (*signifying under his cloak*). But ze pant! it isn't not posseeble zat I find hare. I put hare in von can for de soup and (*growing excited*) sapr-r-riment vare she go—ze pant? (*uttering cry of agony*) Pfui! zare he come *encore!*

PROFESSOR W. (*routing about at the same time as* CAPTAIN FORTINBRAS). Donner Wetter! I cannot mine instrooment find. (*coming down*) Ach-a, ach! vare is mine baro-mater—Autch! (*as if seized again with a stitch.*)

The GUIDES *spread rugs on the snow at* L., *and* CAPTAIN B., PROFESSOR W., *and* CAPTAIN F. *seat themselves after great exertion on the ground, and commence dinner.*

During the following scenes the parties at dinner express by bye-play the difficulties of an Alpine pic-nic—such as (1) *there being a deficiency of water, and the* GUIDES *having to melt snow in a stew-pan over the fire, in order to procure a sufficient supply—the wood to feed the fire being taken from the bundles of small sticks and twigs that are strapped on top of each of the knapsacks littering the stage;* (2) *the want of a corkscrew, and the* PROFESSOR *having to knock off the necks of the wine and beer-bottles with his geological hammer—leathern cups being used for glasses, and each person taking his own drinking vessel out of his pocket;* (3) *that the knives and forks have been forgotten, and that either clasp-knives or fingers must be resorted to;* (4) *that the candles have been packed inside the coffee-pot, and that the lemonade has all burst.*

These, and such other incidents as might be likely to occur under similar circumstances, are intended to be signified by pantomine, and the gestures to be continued at intervals until the repast is finished.

Enter LORD SILVERSPOON, *in knickerbocker suit, Alpine hat, and green veil hat thrown back over it—from cabin* R.

LORD S. (*languidly*). Stiffish pull, isn't it? Takes it out of one more than a scrimmage at foot-ball, and barks your shins much worse, by jingo! (*tries to rub his legs, but can't stoop for stiffness*). I must have lost ten pounds if I dropped an ounce coming over that greasy glacier. But exhausted nature requires a restorative; so I shall go in for a pull at the beer (*attempts to move, and is seized with a stitch*). Oh, good morning! (*sits down with difficulty in front of fire on one of the rugs, and beckons* GUIDE *to bring him a bottle of beer.*)

Enter CHIRPEY *from behind cabin.*

CHIRPEY. But where's the beloved partner of my four-poster, and the rest of the Chignons? I'll soon have the pet does out of that ramshackle rabbit-hutch (*goes and knocks at front window of the cabin*). Anybody at home?

FLORENCE (*sliding back the sash, and putting out her head covered with a cambric handkerchief*). Here I am, Daddy dear!

CHIRPEY (*kissing her*). Bless her! she looks as fresh as an Alpine rhododendron (*goes to back of fire*).

Act II.   MONT BLANC.   29

Enter FLORENCE *and* MISS JETSAM. *They are attired in regular Alpine costumes.*

FLORENCE (*as she comes out of cabin-door supporting* MISS J., *and crosses to* C.). What, sitting down to dinner, gentlemen, without the ladies! I was told there were no bears in these parts. (*All attempt to rise, but are unable to do so from stiffness; and give vent to a series of painful exclamations as they strive to get up.*)

CHIRPEY (*pointing admiringly to* FLORENCE *from* R. C.). There's a prop of one's declining years to be proud of! She's a regular chip of the old block—the very image of her father! A'n't you, my dear? (*chucks her under the chin*). Like her father, bless her! she's as lively as a two-year-old (*tries to be skittish, but is seized with a sharp pain in the attempt*). Oh, crikey! (*crosses to fire, spreads his coat out, and warms himself.*)

FLORENCE (*runs to* MISS J., *and brings her down*). Come, Carry! never say die!

MISS J. Ah, Florence dear! I'm not so strong as you are. You always delighted in hardy exercises. You're not like a girl.

FLORENCE. (*bringing down* MISS J.). No! I never was one of your milksop, lackadaisical ladies, who love to dream their young days away, lolling on a sofa, with a vinaigrette in one hand and the last new sentimental novel in the other. I'm not one of your modern Misses who wish to be thought interesting—who (*imitating their manner*) are so delicate—so excitable—and so gushing—who doat upon lap-dogs and call babies "awful little bores"—who love to display their charity and elegant costumes at fashionable and philanthropic fancy-fairs, and never fail to turn their back upon their poor relations. No, Carry! I'm not like such girls. I was a tom-boy in the nursery—an unruly romp at school—and have been a fly-away mad cap ever since. Give me a pair of sculls and a light boat—a fly-rod and a good trout-stream—a rattling burst with the hounds, and a clear country—and I'll show you what a thorough-bred English girl can do against all the maudlin maidens in the world. There! after that little burst of feeling, let's have some dinner.

MISS J. But won't you wait for your Mama, Florence dear?

CHIRPEY. Ay! that reminds me the old lady's got the table-cloth for a sheet (*goes to the cabin-window, taps at it, as he stands on a stone, and puts his ear to the easement, as if listening expectantly for the answer from within*). Come along, old girl! What d'ye say? "You're so poorly!" Eh, what? Nonsense! (*derisively*) You can't get a coffin up here. So come out! (*beckons to* GUIDES, *two of whom enter the cabin. Goes to cabin door, and receives* MRS. C. *as she comes out.*)

Enter MRS. CHIRPEY *from cabin* R., *supported by a* GUIDE *on either side, with* CHIRPEY *following. She is in a dreadfully exhausted condition, and enveloped in a railway-rug, with a shawl thrown over her head.*

CHIRPEY. That's it, old woman! I told you we'd have you out (*one of the* GUIDES *retires, and leaves* MRS. C. *clinging closely to the other*). Come, I say, Mrs. Chirpey! You needn't hug that young man *quite* so tight—if you please. If we *are* ten thousand feet above the level of the sea, decency, Madam, must still be observed. (GUIDE *leaves her.*)

MRS. C. (*opening her eyes as with extreme languor, and then closing them again with a shudder, as she looks upon* CHIRPEY). Ugh! you repulsive-looking little wretch! What a fright you've made of yourself. (*crosses to* C.)

CHIRPEY. Come! you're getting yourself again: you're becoming abusive.

MRS. C. Oh, Christopher! this horrid Alpine climbing. I never had such a number of distressing symptoms crowded together in all my many painful illnesses.—Nausea, (*ticking them off on her fingers*)! headache! heartburn! vertigo! faintness! snow-blindness! and suffocation!—all one on top of the other. And even now I feel as if I could drop through the mountain (*is about to sit down on one of the hampers at* L. C.)

CHIRPEY (*rushing at her, and preventing her availing herself of the basket*). Drop through the mountain! you'll drop through on to the bottled beer. Here's a nice soft stone for you (*seating her on the large boulder at* R). There! now I'll go and warm you up a tin of gravy soup (*goes to fire at* L, *and commences heating one of the soup-cans from* L. *over it*).

MRS. C. (*in a sepulchral tone*). Florence, dear! (FLORENCE *runs to* MRS. C., *and places her arm round the old lady's waist*.) They'll never take your poor mother down alive.

FLORENCE (*half-laughing*). Oh, Mammy! Mammy!

MRS. C. Promise me, my girl, if your father should marry again, you'll see that the second Mrs. Chirpey is at least (*with suppressed malice*) a good match for him (Oh! my poor back). And you'll take care that my remains (Oh! my poor bones!) are taken to Kensall Green—and you'll make your father put up "deeply lamented," and add, "Affliction sore—long time I bore—Physicians"—wher-ever is the soup?

CHIRPEY (*crossing to* MRS. C., *and hobbling up with a tin and a spoon*). Here, my heart's comforter! this 'll bring the colour back to your cheeks (*puts a spoonful into her mouth*). MRS. C. *makes a wry face, gives a shudder, and pushes* CHIRPEY *from her*.) What's the matter? It's the very best gravy. (*tastes it himself, spits it out, flings the can off* R.C., *and clutches his stomach*.) Bring the colour back to her cheek! I should think it would! Why, it's paint! (*shuddering, as he throws tin off* R. 1 E.), and very bad paint, too.

CAPTAIN F. (*starting up*). Pant! Zousand nams of ze zunders! he cook ma pant, and zen zrow hare avay. Vat is ze brosse vizout ze pant! I vill go circulate myself for hare. *Exit* R. 1 E.

MISS J. (*who has already come to the side of* MRS. C.). I'm sure you will be better indoors, Mrs. Chirpey.

MRS. C. Dear, kind soul! Take me into the cabin, do! and let me breathe my last in peace.

Exit MRS. C., *led by* MISS J. *and* GUIDE *into cabin* R. CHIRPEY *and* FLORENCE *cross over to* L., *and join the party at dinner* L.

Enter HAROLD MAJORIBANKS *through trap* L. C.

HAROLD M. (*coming down* L. C.) Soh! all bids fair! The mist is rising up the valley; and the snow on the Montets is like white marble (*bows as he passes the party at dinner*). Loss of appetite, they say, is one of the symptoms induced by Alpine climbing. I am glad to see that you, ladies and gentlemen, are bent on demolishing the chickens and the theory.

CHIRPEY (*brandishing the leg of a fowl*). Yes; you see I'm trying to beat the march with a drumstick.

FLORENCE (*laughing, and holding up a wing*). And *I'm* trying, Mr. Majoribanks, whether a wing will help me up.

ACT II. MONT BLANC.

HAROLD M. (*with a bow to* FLORENCE). Beings "ever bright and fair" need no extraneous wings to make *them* mount the skies. (*Aside*) Umph! I flatter myself Centlivre couldn't touch *that*. But (*looking round*) where the deuce *is* he? (*crossing to cabin-window*). Come, Percy! here's the dinner going on. Look alive! I've finished my rations an hour ago.

Enter CENTLIVRE *from cabin* R.

CENTLIVRE. So have I—and was having a snooze after it (*sits down on the boulder at* R. 1 E., *and stretches his legs well out*).
HAROLD M. Well, old fellow! We've given our governors the slip and opened the campaign.
CENTLIVRE. Yes; the battle's begun—as briskly as if we were the deadliest of foes.
HAROLD M. And yet the best of friends.
CENTLIVRE. Speak low! She's there, remember.
HAROLD M. I don't forget her, rest assured.
CENTLIVRE (*confidentially; he has beckoned to his side* HAROLD M., *who puts one foot upon the boulder, and, resting his arm on his knee, leans over, so that he may listen the more readily*). Do you know, Harold, while we were clambering through the steep forest of "*Les Pélerins*" this morning, and I caught a glimpse of Florence smiling so sweetly on you as you led her mule along, I had serious thoughts of beating a retreat, and leaving you master of the field?
HAROLD M. Curious! For when you, Percy, shot on ahead to order milk and wild strawberries for her breakfast at the "*Châlet de la Pera*," and I heard her thank you so prettily for your forethought, I had the idea of making the same sacrifice (*sighs*). But then I looked once more upon her lovely face!
CENTLIVRE (*rapturously*). And was there ever such loveliness?
HAROLD M. She's as full of life and grace as the chamois.
CENTLIVRE. As pure and fair as Mont Blanc's crowning snow.
HAROLD M. Yes! (*pauses*) And, therefore, I remained.
CENTLIVRE. Well, its all in our programme.
HAROLD M. Ay; the war between us was to be a *civil* one. But I must go and watch for the return of the pioneers. You'd better come with me, Cent. (*going up* R., CENTLIVRE *following*). There's no chance of parleying with the pretty prisoner whilst the governor (*pointing to* CHIRPEY) keeps watch and ward. So let's retire (*offering* CENTLIVRE *his cigar-case*) to smoke the calumet of peace.

Exeunt HAROLD M., *and* CENTLIVRE, *by trap* L. C.

CHIRPEY (*rising with difficulty*). Well, the inner-man's a trifle better (*stroking his waistcoat*), but the exterior scoundrel (*stroking his limbs*) is still very shaky. (*to* FLORENCE, *who has helped him to rise, and as he hobbles along on her arm to door of cabin*) Do you know, my dear (*halts*), your poor father's body feels as if it had just come home from the wash, and all his bones had been well mangled, his muscles stiffly starched, and his sinews thoroughly ironed?

Exeunt CHIRPEY *and* FLORENCE *into cabin* R.

CAPTAIN B. (*rising with* PROFESSOR W., *as if after a long argument with him*). Tell that to the Marines, Sir! Gold found in these rocks! Pshaw! I don't care who you say found it. I tell you its a downright imposition, Sir. Get gold out of 'em? Stuff and nonsense! you can't get a brass farthing out of 'em, sir. (*goes up* C.)
PROFESSOR W. Vil you mit me gome? (*goes up* L.) and I vill gif you demonstraatseeown. I have mine hammer, and mine plow-bibe (*pro-*

ducing them), and mit your own eyes you shall it drough mine meecroscoope, see? *Exeunt* CAPTAIN B. *and* PROFESSOR W., L. 2 E.

GUIDES *lie down on rugs to sleep.*

LORD S. (*rising, with bag of prunes in his hand*). A'n't these prunes plummy? Best things, they say, to climb on. (*Moves, languidly and yawning, towards cabin-door*, R.)

Enter MISS JETSAM *from cabin* R.

MISS J. (*to herself as entering*). Cold as the air is, it's quite refreshing after the stifling atmosphere of that cabin. (*meeting* LORD S.) Taking your dessert, my Lord?

LORD S. Ye-es. What's a fellah to do? The only amusements possible in such a place are eating and sleeping. Awfully slow up here, isn't it? (*after a pause*) I say, Miss Jetsam, were you ever in love? (*offering bag to her*) Have a prune?

MISS J. (*taking one, and laughing*). In love, my Lord? what a curious question! Suppose I answer it by another. (*pauses*) Were you?

LORD S. Oh, ye-es, scores of times. Spooning's very good fun—and all that sort of thing. But it wants variety. After all, you know, it's only the same feeling over and over again. (*offering her the bag*) You'd better have another. (*crosses behind to window of cabin* R.)

MISS J. (*shaking her head*). Then I suppose your Lordship is suffering from a surfeit of the sweet-stuff. (*sits on boulder*, R.)

LORD S. (*going to the side of the cabin, and beginning to cut his name on the shutter with his penknife*). Oh, no! I'm uncommonly fond of Cupid's confectionery; though, perhaps, the artful little pastry-cook *is* apt to lay the sugar on rather too thick about the bride-cake.

MISS J. (*with covert sarcasm*). Indeed. Love to you, then—as to most venerable philosophers—is a mere hollow vanity?

LORD S. (*carving and dropping chips from his hand*). Ye-es. A pretty, rainbow-tinted bubble, whose very existence is due to—so much "*soft soap.*"

MISS J. Then, I suppose, Lord Silverspoon has closed his heart against the tender passion?

LORD S. Oh, no! Haven't put the shutters up yet (*pauses, and continues carving*). The business carried on as usual during the alterations.

MISS J. You don't say so? May-be, a new tenant has taken possession of the desirable premises.

LORD S. Ye-es; and on a long lease too.

MISS J. It might appear rude if I were to ask the name; but you know a woman's inquisitiveness.

LORD S. Ye-es. That's the old curiosity shop. So you want to know the name? Try and guess.

MISS J. I never could solve a riddle in my life.

LORD S. I've linked the name here with my own.

MISS J. (*going towards him on his left*). Oh, *do* let me see! Who *is* the beauty?

LORD S. (*covering the inscription with his hand*). It's one that is very difficult to cut out, I can tell you.

MISS J. I promise you I won't be jealous.

LORD S. Sure you can't guess?

MISS J. (*shaking her head*). Sure; and, therefore, I must *see* (*pulls him away—looks at the name—and then boxes his ears*). Oh, you impudent young monkey! *Exit* MISS JETSAM *into cabin*, R.

LORD S. (*rubbing his face*). I suppose that was intended for my cheek. (*goes up* C.)

Act II.   MONT BLANC.   33

Enter CENTLIVRE, *stamping his feet, and chafing his hands, by trap,* L.O.

Cousin Cent., by jingo! I've spotted *his* little game! I'll get behind the rocks and watch the fun.

Exit LORD S. *behind rock near masked trap,* C.

CENTLIVRE. I've had enough of that looking out yonder for the Guides, so I'll just look out here a bit for myself. (*glancing around*) Every one asleep! but *I* can't rest for the thoughts of Florence.

Enter FLORENCE *from cabin,* R.

Lime-light throws a golden tint over the scene.

FLORENCE (*laughing as she goes to cabin window-shutter*). I must see what that precocious little wretch has been doing about Carry. (*looking at corner of cabin*) Oh, here it is! I declare if he hasn't cut out their two initials, and enclosed 'em in a heart. What *will* those boys be thinking about next?

CENTLIVRE (*aside*). There she is. Now is my opportunity (*approaching her*). Has Miss Florence come to enjoy the beauty of the Alpine sunset? See yonder (*pointing to the distance*) how the sinking orb of day begins to change the silver of the mountain tops into peaks of burnished gold?

FLORENCE. Why, Mr. Centlivre, you're quite poetical (*laughs and crosses to him.*)

LORD S. *peeps from behind the rocks, and rubs his hands with glee.*

CENTLIVRE. In such a shower of gold came Jupiter of old to woo the lovely Danäe.

FLORENCE. I left my heathen mythology behind me when I quitted school (*crosses* L.). But it seems from what you say that the ancient deities who delighted to pay their addresses in showers of gold (*laughing*) knew well how to approach a lady under the most favourable auspices. (*goes to* R. *of fire*).

CENTLIVRE (*aside*). I wonder whether she's chaffing me now! (*to* FLORENCE) Amidst such majestic peaks and pinnacles as these, the soul shakes off the dust of earth, and, soaring heavenwards, stands trembling on the confines of the realms of love.

LORD S. *mimics his gestures.*

FLORENCE. Very pretty, I'm sure, Mr. Centlivre! but (*laughing again*) I can't help thinking—if this chilly region be anywhere near the realms you speak of—the love which dwells there must be very cold (*shivers*).

CENTLIVRE (*aside* L. C.). There must be *some* inlet to her heart. (*To* FLORENCE.) But true love, Miss Florence, is neither chilled by cold nor seared by heat. Even as the enduring violet—it blooms alike in snow and sunshine.

FLORENCE. Really, Mr. Centlivre, what with violets and sunshine—gods and goddesses—showers of gold, and realms of love—you seem to possess a fair share of the gems necessary for a modern poet's glittering stock-in-trade (*laughs*).

CENTLIVRE. Still laughing! and no wonder, when smiles can make the pearly teeth add the same beauty to those coral lips as glistening dewdrops lend to parted rose-leaves. (*He comes down* C.)

FLORENCE. There! there! If you're going on in that way, Mr. Centlivre, I certainly must try to be serious. See! now I'm as solemn as a muffled drum. But mind! I can't promise to remain long so. (*bursts out laughing again*) You really must excuse me! I know it's very rude! but you *do* look *so* spooney! (*goes to him.*)

D

LORD S. *is convulsed.*
CENTLIVRE (*in an impassioned tone*). Do not—I implore you—trifle with me any longer. Hear me tell you in this solemn wilderness of snow—with nothing but the everlasting skies above us, and the transitory world far below at our feet—hear me tell you, Florence! (*seizes her hand.*)
FLORENCE (*startled*). Mr. Centlivre!
CENTLIVRE. I love you!
FLORENCE (*remonstratingly*). Mr. Centlivre!
CENTLIVRE (*desperately*). Hand—heart—fortune—life—all shall be given up to you!
FLORENCE (*struggling to withdraw her hand*). Mr. Centlivre!
CENTLIVRE (*solemnly*). Hear me swear——

LORD SILVERSPOON *puts his head in front of the spur of the* 1ST MULET, *and pushes away a large piece of the rock, which falls upon the stage with a loud crash, and reveals a masked-trap, representing a snow-covered crevasse behind it*—LORD S. *disappears.*

CENTLIVRE. Damnation! (*goes* L.)
FLORENCE *bursts away from him, and exit into cabin* R.
GUIDES *startled by noise, rise from sleeping.*

CENTLIVRE (*pacing the stage angrily*). The very rocks conspire to crush my love. Some avalanche must have fallen hard-by to smother the sweet confession that was trembling on her lips. But oh, cursed fate! (*shaking his fist above his head*) why should it be destined to fall at the most precious moment of my life?

Exit CENTLIVRE *into cabin* R.

GUIDES *curl themselves down again on rugs to sleep.*

LORD S. *puts his head out from behind the crags, imitates* CENTLIVRE'S *action of shaking his fist in the air, and then, convulsed with inward laughter, buries his face in his hands.*

Enter HAROLD M., *with* FRANÇOIS *and* 2ND GUIDE, *by trap* R. C.
Limelight changes to a rosy tint.

HAROLD M. (*talking as he enters*). Good! The bridges of ice are sound you say. But the wind is rising, is it not? (*noise of fresh breeze without.*)
FRANÇOIS (*at* R.) These are but a few puffs common at sundown. As the moon gets up, the breeze is sure to lull. The morning sun will see us plant our bâtons on the summit of Mont Blanc. (*discovers* LORD S. *on the crags, and shouts anxiously to him*). Young Milor! young Milor! What are you doing there? One step backward, and you are lost! The snow behind you is but a film over a deep crevasse (*pointing to masked trap at* C.)
HAROLD M. Come away, youngster! Don't you hear: your life's not worth a moment's purchase! (*goes up, and then comes down* L.)
LORD S. *descends the rock sulkily, and saunters into cabin carelessly—with his hands in his pockets, and whistling as he goes.* Exit LORD S. *at* L.

FRANÇOIS *and* 2ND GUIDE *go to the fire, and commence preparing some of the eatables for their supper.*

HAROLD M. (*crossing over to the side of cabin*). Well! I little thought when I carved my name on these planks, two autumns ago, that

Harold Majoribanks would figure again in the Chamouni lists among the candidates for mountain "honours." Nor should *I* were it not for the sake of her for whose safety I would gladly risk my life. But I can't dissuade her from braving the hardships and perils of the ascent. So *go* I must!

Enter CHIRPEY *from cabin* R.

CHIRPEY. It's no use my trying to sleep! Sleep's like a widow: if she means to knobble you, she does'nt want much wooing (*meeting* HAROLD M.) Halloa, Mr. Majoribanks! Well! do you still intend to have a cut at that magnificent iced-pudding yonder? (*pointing to distant mountain*). But you've been over the ground before, you say. And is the rest of the road in the same excellent state of repair as the remarkable piece of paving we've just travelled over?

HAROLD M. (*laughing*). That's a mere flea-bite to the difficulties to come.

CHIRPEY. Oh, thank you! Such flea-bites are too ticklish by far for me. And you're still resolved on going up, are you? (HAROLD *nods and smiles*) Then allow me to make you a confidential communication (*looks round, and then stands on tiptoes as he whispers in his ear*) I'm not! I've had enough of it. (*Aside*) Umph! a thought strikes me! (HAROLD M. *goes and speaks to* FRANÇOIS, *who is at* L., *while* CHIRPEY *speaks his aside*.) He seems an extremely obliging young man—I'll get him to put my bill of the "Persuasive Pickles" up on the summit for me. (*to* HAROLD M. *blandly*) Mr. Majoribanks, Sir! I'm proud to know you (*they shake hands*). I admire your determination and your genuine British pluck; and I'm going to ask you—if I may make so bold—to do me a particular favour.

HAROLD M. Anything that lies in my power, Mr. Chirpey, I'm sure I shall be only too happy to——

CHIRPEY (*with enthusiasm*). You'll excuse me, Sir, taking the liberty with you, but (*impulsively slapping him on the back*) you're a deuced fine young fellow (*glances round cautiously to assure himself that no one is listening*), and I want you to take a pretty little thing of mine up to the top of Mont Blanc for me.

HAROLD M. (*aside*). He's about to place his daughter under my protection! (*to* CHIRPEY). I can but assure you, Mr. Chirpey, I feel highly honoured by the confidence you repose in me.

CHIRPEY. Nobly spoken, Sir! What I'm about to hand over to you is a little thing I've set my heart upon for many a day.

HAROLD M. No doubt you have, Mr. Chirpey! no doubt!

CHIRPEY. Do credit to any man. All my own creation, too! And, what's more, a perfect picture.

HAROLD M. Ay! a picture (*rapturously*) that Raffaelle himself might be proud to copy.

CHIRPEY. So he might, Sir! No vulgar gaudy and tricky bit of goods; but got up in first-rate style.

HAROLD M. Certainly!

CHIRPEY (*going to one of the knapsacks lying on the ground at* R., *and unstrapping a long roll from the top of it—Noise of wind without*). I'm about to place in your hands, Mr. Majoribanks, the anxious thought of a life-time.

Enter CAPTAIN FORTINBRAS *by entrance from below* L. 1 E.

CAPTAIN F. Ma pant! I can't nevare see hare—no vare! (*looks about, as if still searching for it.*)

CHIRPEY (*bringing forward the roll, and handing it to* HAROLD M.— *much to his astonishment*). Take it, Sir, and place it on that lofty and

D 2

noble pinnacle which alone is a fitting shrine for so elevated and grand an idea.

CAPTAIN F. (*starting at the words*). How? Vat is zat he say? Grande idday! I vill keep myself a leetel secret (*hides behind the crags up* R. C.).

HAROLD M. (*unfolding the bill and regarding it with disgust*). What's this? "Shah's Delight!" And to be put up on top of Mont Blanc! Oh, I see it all now! Confound it! he wants to make a bill-sticker of me, instead of the protector of his daughter (*lets the bill fall from his hands in his amazement*).

CAPTAIN F. (*coming down from* R. C., *snatching up bill, running up behind masked trap* C., *and shaking his fist in the air*). Sacr-r-re! I have seen him! I vill have his blood for zis.

Noise of wind without.

CHIRPEY (*running after* CAPTAIN F.). Stop him! stop him! Oh, lor'! oh, lor'! I wouldn't lose that bit of paper for worlds. I'll have it, if I die for it (*rushes up* L., *and gets behind rock*).

HAROLD M. Hold hard! not that way!

FRANÇOIS (*starting up*). Beware of the crevasse!

HAROLD M. It's right before you! He'll be lost! (*rushes after him*).

CAPTAIN F. *brandishes bill above his head, and, seeing* CHIRPEY *following him, throws it down entrance trap* C., *and then exit* L. 3 E.

CHIRPEY, *in pursuit of* CAPTAIN F., *on reaching the crags, which are a continuation of the back spurs of* 1ST MULET, *stumbles over the stone that* LORD SILVERSPOON *had thrown down, and is seen to fall bodily through the sheet of tissue-paper covering the trap at* C., *and the moment after a cloud of snow is sent up high into the air.*

FRANÇOIS (*shouting to those asleep*). Wake up! to the rescue! Man in the crevasse!

GUIDES *start up and get ropes.* MRS. CHIRPEY, FLORENCE, MISS JETSAM, LORD SILVERSPOON, *and* CENTLIVRE *hurry on, with a frightened look, from the cabin.*

During the general commotion which ensues, HAROLD *seizes a rope, makes a nooze to it, and passes it under his arms.*

HAROLD M. (*authoritatively*). Keep back there! Be still! Here, quick, François! (*gives* GUIDES *the rope*) Steady all of you! Remember you have *my* life, as well as *his*, in your hands.

HAROLD *descends into the trap.* GUIDES *keep paying out rope.* FRANÇOIS *runs up the rock, and, mounting one of the spurs, peeps down from it into the crevasse.*

MRS. CHIRPEY *faints in the arms of* LORD SILVERSPOON, MISS JETSAM *covers her face with her hands, and leans on* CENTLIVRE's *shoulder—whilst* FLORENCE *follows* FRANÇOIS *up the spur of the rock, and stations herself by his side, and seems to be looking anxiously down below.*

FRANÇOIS (*giving directions to* GUIDES *at edge of crevasse*). Easy there!

FLORENCE. Oh! for pity's sake! take care.

FRANÇOIS. Now pay away! give him plenty of rope.

FLORENCE. Stop! he's near my dear father now.

FRANÇOIS. That's enough! Easy, lads, easy! Steady, don't let the rope jerk so.

FLORENCE (*turning her head away*). How terribly he sways from side to side.

FRANÇOIS. Stop! he waves his hand! stop I say!

FLORENCE (*with a shriek of delight*). Thank Heaven! he has my father in his arms! See, François! see!
FRANÇOIS. Here they come!
FLORENCE. Noble fellow! he's saved my father!
   SILVERSPOON *throws his hat in the air.*
FRANÇOIS. Now quick! pull away! all of you! Pull with a will!

   (*All this passes very rapidly.*)

HAROLD *appears with* CHIRPEY *in his arms at the mouth of the trap* C. FRANÇOIS *takes* CHIRPEY (*covered with snow*) *from him, lays him on the stage on a rug,* R. *side of fire, and supports his head on his knee.* HAROLD *springs on to the rocks, throws off the rope, and comes down amid the general cheers of the* GUIDES, *who cluster round him, shake him by the hand, and pat him on the back.*

FLORENCE (*kneeling* R. *side of* CHIRPEY). Speak to me, Daddy dear! (*to* FRANÇOIS) How pale he looks! Let me loosen his cravat.
HAROLD M. (*at* R.) Give him a sup from my flask (*hands flask to* FRANÇOIS —FLORENCE *takes it from him and puts it to* CHIRPEY's *lips.*)
CHIRPEY *opens his eyes, groans dismally, and then shuts them again.*
MRS. C. (*breaking away from* CENTLIVRE). My poor dear husband! Thank Heaven, he lives! (*to* HAROLD M.) And I would thank you too, Mr. Harold, but (*bursting into tears*) I can't as I ought — for my heart's in my mouth.
FLORENCE (*crossing to* HAROLD M. *with emotion*). I owe my father's life to you, Mr. Majoribanks; (CENTLIVRE *crosses behind* HAROLD M.) and his daughter, rest assured, will remember your noble conduct as long as she lives—yes! as long as she lives!
HAROLD *bows.*
CENTLIVRE (*aside,* R. *of* HAROLD). A death-blow that to all my hopes. (*to* HAROLD) You've won the battle, Harold, fairly; aye, and nobly too!
LORD S. (*slapping* HAROLD *on the back*). Majoribanks, you're a trump! and what more can one man say to another? (HAROLD *laughs, and returns his slap on the shoulder.*)
CHIRPEY (*sitting up and rubbing his head*). Florence! (*she runs and kneels down by his side* R.) Bless her! (*stroking her cheek*) I thought I'd left you for ever, my girl, but I'm not hurt, only dazed (*waving his hand before his eyes*). Your poor old father's better now; there's life in the old dog yet (*rises, and* MRS. C. *gets on his* L. *side*).
FLORENCE. Oh, I'm so glad (*kisses him*). And we owe all to Mr. Harold, Daddy dear.
CHIRPEY (*shaking himself, as if to collect his senses*). Was it he, then, that saved me? Where is he? (HAROLD *advances*) Give me your hand, Mr. Harold; no, let me call you Harold after this (*continues shaking him by the hand a longish time, and then rises by the aid of it*). I never was much of a dab at speech-making—I can't manage any fine phrases, but, until this heart grows cold in Chirpey's bosom, you shall always have a nice warm corner in it.
FLORENCE (*tenderly*). But won't you come into the cabin, Dad?
CHIRPEY. No, no! Do you go in and take the others with you. I want to be quiet, and the air will do me good.
MRS. C. Ah, Chirpey! thank Goodness you're safe! There isn't much of you, but I shouldn't like to lose what there is—especially now I'm so poorly.

Exeunt FLORENCE, MRS. CHIRPEY, MISS JESTAM, LORD S., HAROLD, *and* CENTLIVRE *into cabin.*

CHIRPEY (*clasping his head in his hands*). My head feels as if it was stuffed with cotton-wool. Old age is very like old port—it can't stand much shaking without—let me see, what was I going to say? without its getting—a—yes, that's it!—as dreadfully muddled as I am at the present moment (*sits R. of fire*).

Enter CAPTAIN FORTINBRAS, PROFESSOR WINDBEUTEL, *and* CAPTAIN BROADSIDE, *from behind rocks*, L. 3 E.

CAPTAIN B. (*at C., to* FORTINBRAS, *as he enters*). I tell you, Sir, that if any countryman of mine has insulted you, he'll only be too happy to give you the satisfaction one gentleman expects from another.

CAPTAIN F. (*at R., excitedly*). He cook ma pant! Dee-able! Vat for he cook ma pant? I tell him I come here for to place ze nam of ma naschione on ze Mont Blanc top, and zen I hear him say he vant to place von affix of his detestaable peekel on ze top of hare too! Zousand nams of ze zunders! Ansoolt ma naschione sare—ansoolt me myself.

PROFESSOR W. *Ja wohl!* De Herr Gabitaine has right. *Preemo.* (*ticking it off on his fingers*). De opsticking of de meex peekel bill von colossa-al scanda-al is. *Segundo.* De paint-taking for de soup-making a never-to-be-outwashed-midout-bloodletting degradatsiown is. *Tertio*——

CAPTAIN B. (*interrupting the* PROFESSOR). Belay there! take a round turn with that long yarn, will you? (*To* CHIRPEY.) Mr. Chirpey, this gentleman says you have insulted him, and he demands satisfaction.

CHIRPEY (*rising grandly and going* L. C.). Sir, as an enlightened British tradesman, it is Christopher Chirpey's constant endeavour to give *general* satisfaction.

CAPTAIN B. He insists on a meeting immediately on your return to Chamouni; and I, acting as your friend in the matter. have taken upon myself to say that you will be only too happy to attend to his orders.

CHIRPEY (*still wandering, and endeavouring to collect himself*). Attend to his orders! Certainly; one of the main features of my business has always been, "orders punctually attended to" (*sits R. of fire*).

CAPTAIN B. (*aside*). What's the matter with the man? Is he drunk? (*to Chirpey*) You understand, Mr. Chirpey, the nature of the business?

CHIRPEY (*rambling*). Of course he does. And C. C. "hopes, by conducting the business on a principle of the strictest commercial integrity, to ensure a continuance of similar favours."

CAPTAIN B. Then, Sir, you leave the conduct of the affair in my hands; and I shall therefore retire with the Herr Professor here to settle the place and time of meeting.

Exit CAPTAIN B. *into cabin*, R.

PROFESSOR W. (*raising his hat to* CHIRPEY). I make to myself the broudness to take mine head off to you. Lif you vell, mein Herr! (*Aside.*) Ja! lif you vell (*significantly*) for a vile.

Exit PROFESSOR, R.

CAPTAIN F. (*making an elaborate bow to* CHIRPEY). Sare, I have ze honnare you to sal-lute. (*aside*) By ze blue! I will fricassay his goose for him!

Exit CAPTAIN FORTINBRAS, R.

CHIRPEY (*still rubbing his head, and wandering*). What's it all mean? (*calling to* GUIDES, L.) Here, you Guides, give us a pull at the brandy bottle, and let's see whether that will sweep the cobwebs out of my upper-story.

2ND GUIDE *pours out small leathern cupful of Cognac, and* CHIRPEY *tosses it down.*

ACT II.   MONT BLANC.   39

Enter CENTLIVRE *from cabin*, R.

Ah, that's better! The mist's beginning to clear off. I can remember I fell through the snow—yes, and it was Mr. Harold—no, no! I asked him to let me call him Harold; and I told him that, until this heart—ay, it's all coming back! (*rises*).

CENTLIVRE (*at* C.). I'm glad to find that you're yourself again, Mr. Chirpey.

CHIRPEY (*at* L. C.). Yes. But where's your friend?

CENTLIVRE. Oh, Harold is with François in the cabin, arranging the lanterns and the ropes for the ascent to-night.

CHIRPEY. Ah, he's a fine young fellow! and a great favourite with my wife and daughter.

CENTLIVRE. But you can tell how noble is his nature, Mr. Chirpey, by his brave conduct to yourself; for without him you know——

CHIRPEY. Certainly, certainly; it was extremely polite of him.

CENTLIVRE (*astonished*). Polite!

CHIRPEY. Of course it was. Why, you surely don't want to detract from the merit of the action?

CENTLIVRE. I! (*aside*) It strikes me he's rather inclined to do so.

CHIRPEY. But, between ourselves, the service he rendered me wasn't quite so great as the ladies, no doubt, would like to make out.

CENTLIVRE. Indeed!

CHIRPEY. They are always inclined to exaggerate so—you know what women are. As luck would have it, I fell on to a ledge of snow, and, with great presence of mind, I held on to it, like a limpet to a rock; and so, of course, with merely the assistance of a simple rope, I could have clambered up and saved myself.

CENTLIVRE (*aside*). Umph! I see! He'll make out by-and-bye that Majoribanks' services were of no use to him. Oh, vanity! vanity!

CHIRPEY. But, as I said before, until this heart grows cold in Chirpey's bosom—you remember the observation, so I needn't trouble you by repeating the reminder. You understand? (*goes up*).

CENTLIVRE. Yes, I understand! (*aside*) well enough! So then, Majoribanks, you've not won the battle yet. The daughter may be impressed, but the father, clearly, is untouched. I shall stay and fight it out.

Limelight throws a tint of " bright transparent crimson " upon the mountain tops, as well as upon the upper part of the spurs of the two Mulets; and, as the following scene proceeds, the tints keep gradually changing and passing through the several hues of the spectrum, until, at the end of the scene, they assume a rich violet colour. These ultimately subside into the more sombre effect of twilight, amid which the last scene is to take place; while the concluding tableaux, representing the commencement of the night ascent, is to be shown under the effect of the brightest moonlight—the stars and moon upon the cloth at the back of the stage being all lighted up, and the limelight thrown full upon the GUIDES *and characters as they begin to ascend the steep side of the Glacier. For description of the peculiarities of Alpine sunset and moonlight, see* ALBERT SMITH'S " MONT BLANC," *p.* 240.

I have a thought! I'll play my cards into the father's hand.

CHIRPEY (*pointing to distance*). Holloa! It's sunset, and the Guides tell me they rather pride themselves on their sunsets up here.

CENTLIVRE (*going to* CHIRPEY). A stroll in the evening air will do you good. I'll give you my arm, and we'll go and watch the varying tints from the other Mulets yonder (*pointing to* 2ND MULET).

MONT BLANC. ACT II.

CHIRPEY (*coming down and drawing back, as* CENTLIVRE *offers his arm*). No, I thank you. I won't budge an inch again without a Guide. The earth's crust in these parts is a shade too light and flakey to suit my taste.

2ND GUIDE (*down* L. *and coming forward, bowing*). I shall be happy to accompany the gentlemen; along this track there is nothing to fear (*pointing to entrance from below*).

CENTLIVRE *and* GUIDE *take* CHIRPEY *between them*.

CHIRPEY (*to* GUIDE, *as they prepare to descend by trap*). Well, I'm in your hands; and remember, young man, although I've every desire to witness the performance (*going up* L. C.), I'd rather pay for a place in the gallery up there (*pointing to* 2ND MULET), than be passed into the pit (*pointing to crevasse*).

Exeunt CHIRPEY, CENTLIVRE, *and* 2ND GUIDE, *by trap* L. C.

Enter HAROLD M. *and* FLORENCE *from cabin* R., *talking as they come on.*

FLORENCE. Before others I could not thank you as I wished.

HAROLD M. (*confusedly*). Indeed you overrate my services. What I did was merely what a—what, in fact, a—any—a—(*aside*) These praises quite unman me (*commences in a nervous manner to coil down a rope*).

FLORENCE. Do you know, Mr. Majoribanks, the occurrence of this evening has taught me that, although I may have somewhat of a man's love of adventure, still at heart I am but a poor weak woman. Your heroic conduct——

Lights gradually down.

HAROLD M. (*aside*). Oh, I can't stand this! (*to* FLORENCE, *while he is still nervously fiddling with the rope*) Would you oblige me by holding this end while I—while I—a—measure out—or I won't trouble you, as you're engaged just now. I'll call François (*about to move off*).

FLORENCE (*aside*). How indifferent he seems. (*to* HAROLD) Stay, I cannot let you go—I *must* thank you for the life you have given back to us. My love for my father is but the harmony of the chord which has ever vibrated in his bosom for myself. You don't know how good a father he has been! So kind, that he has begotten an affection in my breast which has more of the warmth of human gratitude in it than the mere cold respect of filial duty. And yet, though you have given all this happiness back to me (*tenderly*), you *will* not let me thank you.

HAROLD M. Really, Miss Florence, you distress me. I did no more for him than—a—even you yourself, if I mistake not, would have done.

FLORENCE (*passionately*). Aye, that I would—woman as I am! But you, without any of the love that would have nerved *me* to it, risked *your* life for *my* father's life (*angrily*); and still you will not let me thank you.

HAROLD M. I have told you, Miss Florence, I want no thanks.

FLORENCE (*tearfully*). Why will you thwart this outpouring of my better nature? Even the dog that licks your hand for the bone you give it—thanks you. The beggar that breathes a blessing on your head for the pittance you fling to him—thanks you. And yet you will not let a daughter thank you for the priceless boon of a father's life and love restored! (*buries her face in her hands and bursts into tears.*)

HAROLD M. (*running to her*). You misunderstand me. For Heaven's sake, spare me the misery of those tears! (*tenderly, as he takes her hand and draws her to him, so that she unconsciously drops her head and sobs convulsively upon his shoulder*) Do not, I implore you, Florence!

FLORENCE (*starting back at the word, and amazed as she discovers her position*). What am I doing?

Noise heard without.

CHIRPEY (*calling loudly without*). Here, help! come quick.

Enter CHIRPEY, *by trap from below* R. C., *scrambling up hurriedly and excitedly on to the stage.*

CHIRPEY (*gasping—down* C.). Help! salt! vinegar! pepper! mustard! stretchers! brandy!

FLORENCE (*running to her father*). What has happened, Daddy dear?

CHIRPEY. Don't ask me. Don't speak to me any of you! Frightful accident! (*to* GUIDES) Why the devil don't you stir yourselves?

GUIDES *rush off down trap* L. C.

HAROLD M. (*running to cabin and knocking at the planks at side*). François! make haste! follow me!

Enter FRANÇOIS *from cabin. He is about to rush off with* HAROLD M. *towards the entrance from below, when* CHIRPEY *runs and places himself before them.*

CHIRPEY (*throwing his hands up*). You stop where you are! This is my affair!

Enter CENTLIVRE, *supported by a* GUIDE *on either side, and led on in an apparently fainting condition. Other* GUIDES *follow from trap* L. C. *At the same moment* MRS. CHIRPEY, MISS JETSAM, LORD SILVERSPOON, CAPTAIN BROADSIDE, PROFESSOR WINDBBUTEL, *and* CAPTAIN FORTINBRAS *enter from cabin* R.

MRS. C., MISS J., *and* LORD S. *remain down* R.

CHIRPEY (*in a state of great excitement, as he spreads rug in centre of stage*). Bring him here to me! I saved him! (*He kneels down on it and beckons to* GUIDES *to place* CENTLIVRE *in front of him, so that he may support* CENTLIVRE'S *head upon his knee.* CENTLIVRE *is put on rug in the same position as* CHIRPEY *was*).

ALL. What is it? How did it occur?

2ND GUIDE (*behind fire*). We were——

CHIRPEY (*jumping up, and letting* CENTLIVRE'S *head fall on the snow, in his hurry to stop* 2ND GUIDE). Hold your tongue! Not a word! But for me he would have been a dead man. Rub his temples!

HAROLD M., *who is* R. *of* CENTLIVRE, *and has run to him and propped his friend's head on his knee, is about to give him some liquor out of his flask, when*——

CHIRPEY (*rushing at him, and snatching the flask from his hand*). How dare you, Sir, take that liberty! Nobody shall attend to him but myself (*pushes* HAROLD *away*).

CENTLIVRE (*in a faint voice*). But for the courage of Mr. Chirpey——

CHIRPEY (*rushing up to* CENTLIVRE *and putting his hand over* CENTLIVRE'S *mouth*). No! not you! don't you speak! It's too horrible for you! (*rapidly, and gasping with excitement between the sentences*) Well—we were watching the sunset—when all at once—my poor dear friend would have it he saw my pickle bill that was carried away by that rascally Frenchman—he rushed after it like a noble fellow—I followed.

MRS. C. Like a prudent man.

CHIRPEY (*turning upon her sharply*). Why will you interrupt, when I am working up the excitement? He *would* go after it—when all of a sudden—I saw nothing of him but the soles of his boots—just as he was disappearing down a fearful crevasse. It makes me—boo-ooh! (*shuddering*) shudder even to think of it. Whereupon—with nothing but my native courage to support me—I, Chirpey—the father of a family—whose life is not heavily insured—flew after him.

MRS. CHIRPEY. What imprudence (*returns to* MISS J.)

CHIRPEY (*fiercely*). Woman, would you check the promptings of the noblest feelings of humanity? Then I knelt down at the edge of the yawning abyss—and with the aid of an Alpenstock—and his pulling and my pulling—and our all pulling together—I was enabled, by the blessing of Providence, and a firm grip of his pantaloons—to restore him once more to the face of the earth (*going down* R.).

FLORENCE (*running up to him*). My brave little Dad—bless his dear kind heart! (*kisses him, and crosses to* R. C.).

HAROLD M. Why, Percy! old boy, are you hurt?

CENTLIVRE. Oh, I'm much better now, thank you (*rising and pretending to totter towards* CHIRPEY). And I have to thank you, Sir, more than all. You, Mr. Chirpey, have restored a son to his father.

CHIRPEY (*majestically*). It's true.

CENTLIVRE. Words are powerless to express the gratitude I owe you.

CHIRPEY (*with an air of perfect conviction*). That's true! (*slight pause, and then, as if overcome with emotion*) You've touched my heart, Mr. Percy!—no; let me call you Percy?

CENTLIVRE. With pleasure. (*aside*) It's Percy now, as it was Harold before. Ha! Ha! *Mr.* Harold, I've got the father on my side at last.

HAROLD M. The old shuffler!

CHIRPEY (*feelingly*). Percy. my friend—my son! give me your hand (*shakes him warmly by the hand*). I owe to you the sweetest emotions of my life. Without me you would have been a shapeless mass—repulsive to look upon. You owe everything to me—yes, everything! And (*with great nobility*) I shall never forget it.

CENTLIVRE. Nor I.

CHIRPEY (*to* HAROLD). Ah, young man! (*wiping away a tear*) you don't know the pleasure one experiences in saving a fellow-creature's life.

(*Stars shine out and effect of dusk.*)

FLORENCE. But, Daddy, Mr. Majoribanks is no stranger to the feeling; for you remember——

CHIRPEY. Yes; that's right! Now you remind me, I *do* recollect—(*turning round*) But dear me! what a remarkably-fine night.

FRANCOIS (*coming forward*). Yes, gentlemen, we shall have the moon up shortly. The night promises so fair that, with all respect, I should advise we start as soon as possible.

2ND GUIDE (*up* C.). Thanks to Mr. Harold, the lanterns and ropes are all ready.

Some of the GUIDES *begin collecting the knapsacks, others take provisions out of hampers, and others bring ropes and lanterns from the cabin, whilst others commence to sharpen up the points of the ice-axes with whetstones, and others to test the soundness of the steps of the ice-ladders. One takes a telescope, and, after surveying the landscape, draws the attention of one or two of his comrades to something he has caught sight of below.*

FRANÇOIS. I should like you to be on the "Grand Plateau" before the morning sun has power to soften the snow. And each of you must remem:-

ber to travel as lightly laden as possible; for, bear in mind, the less load the greater the chance of avoiding the dangers of the masked crevasses.

HAROLD M. Ay! the ascent from here will seem comparatively easy; but I, as an old Alpine climber, can tell you that when, in the early morning, we come to scale the steep frozen rampart of the *Mur de la Côte,* we shall have to cut our foot and hand-holds in the ice (*drawing the ice-axe from his side*) as we go—crawling up the towering cliff of glass like flies upon a window-pane.

FRANÇOIS. And now to see how many our party is to number (*takes out note-book and proceeds to write down the names of the ascending party*).

HAROLD. One! (*taps his breast.*)

FLORENCE. Two! (MRS. CHIRPEY *shrieks*)

CENTLIVRE. Three! (HAROLD *starts, and looks at him*)

LORD S. Four!—and, Miss Jetsam, I think five! (*bows to her*)

MISS J. Oh, no! not I, indeed!

CHIRPEY (*crossing to* FRANÇOIS). Nor I! I've had enough of such acrobatic performances. No more ground-and-lofty tumbling for me, thank you! (*aside*) I lost my motive when I lost my pickle-bill.

MRS. C. Nor I!—No! not if I could be taken up in the Lord Mayor's state-carriage!

CAPTAIN B. (*at* R.). Nor I, by Davey Jones! I call it all an infernal imposition! (*crosses to* L.)

PROFESSOR W. (*up C.*). I also not! What to me now are the wonder-beauties of de lovely Natnor—for ach-a! ach-a! ach! I lose mine instrooment! *Der Tueful!* How can I to de height mount midout mine instrooment?

CAPTAIN F. (*up* L.—*savagely*). And me! What for I go? What for I go? Hein! (*aside, drawing himself up, as he looks at* CHIRPEY *with supreme contempt*) Ze old cow of a Jean Bull! He cook ma pa'nt! What for I go? (*goes up stage*).

CHIRPEY (*at* L. C., *taking* CENTLIVRE *aside*). I say, young man! you're never going to make one of the fools. How can you go up with nearly every bone in your body broken?

CENTLIVRE (*at* C., *aside*). Oh! I forgot my accident!

CHIRPEY. Haven't I just saved your life? And here you want to risk it again! I'm not going, and you can't go without me; who's to protect you? (*takes* CENTLIVRE'S *arm*)

CENTLIVRE (*aside, with a groan*). I'm caught in my own trap! He'll see through it all if I venture. Iove says follow the girl. Diplomacy says stick to the father. I'll follow diplomacy (*crosses to* LORD S.).

CAPTAIN B. (*down* L. *of* CHIRPEY, *and taking him aside*). Glad to hear, Sir, you're not going to make an ass of yourself! Remember you're in my hands, Sir, and depend upon it, I wouldn't allow you to run the chance of killing yourself by falling into a hole up there like an idiot. when I've made arrangements for you to distinguish yourself by falling in a duel down below like a gentleman (*walks away from him*).

CHIRPEY (*bewildered, at* L.). Duel! What on earth does he mean? (*crosses to* R.)

CENTLIVRE (*taking* LORD SILVERSPOON *aside*). Look here, Silver! You're going up—I'm not. You can do me a good turn. Just keep your eyes on Harold and Florence! You understand me! and you promise.

LORD S. (*at* R., *imitating* CENTLIVRE'S *action in the previous scene*). Hear me swear!

CENTLIVRE (*astonished*). Umph! What's that? (*then as a flood of light bursts suddenly in upon him*) Oh, you young villian (*rushes at him and shakes him*).

MRS. C. (*to* CHIRPEY, *as she advances* R. *of him, and points to*

FLORENCE, *and throws up her hands in horror at the idea of the girl's going up*). Mr. Chirpey! if you're a man and a father, you'll assert your authority.

CHIRPEY (*pompously*). Leave it to me, Madam! (*to* FLORENCE) Florence! your father objects to this foolery. You've seen what's happened to me —with all my sagacity. Your fond and ever-watchful parent forbids you to go.

FLORENCE (*coming to him and putting her arms round his neck*, C.). Daddy dear! you know I never do anything that you don't approve of. But (*wheedling*) think of the honour if a child of yours should be one of the few women who have conquered the perils of Mont Blanc!

CHIRPEY (*bursting into a smile of pride*). Go along, you little humbug! You women always have your own way.

MRS. C. Except poor me!

During the above, the GUIDES *have called* FRANCOIS *to them, and he has taken the telescope and reconnoitred down below.*

FRANCOIS (*up stage,* C., *to* HAROLD, *as he gives him the glass*). This is not the first time we have been served this shabby trick! Here are two mean fellows taking advantage of our track in the snow. Look through the glass, Sir, and see whether you noticed them at the Hotel at Chamouni.

HAROLD M. (*up stage,* C., *and looking through the glass and then dropping it*). By all that's unfortunate! it's my own father.

CENTLIVRE (*up stage, and snatching up the telescope*). And by all that's unpropitious mine is with him! (*comes down* L.)

HAROLD M. (*to* GUIDES). I did one of you a good turn when I was last here. Do the same now for me! Quick—the ascent!

FRANCOIS (*to* GUIDES). Make haste! the ropes, the lanterns, and the axes! (*to* HAROLD M.) Come with me this way and we shall avoid them.

Exeunt FRANÇOIS *and* 2ND GUIDE, *followed by others, with ropes, lanterns, &c., and accompanied by* HAROLD, FLORENCE, *and* LORD SILVERSPOON.

Enter the EARL OF OSBORNE *and* DR. MAJORIBANKS, *with a* GUIDE, *by trap,* L. C.

DR. M. (*at* R) }
and } Where are they?
EARL OF O. (*at* C.) }

EARL OF O. (*to* CENTLIVRE, *who is at* L.). How dare you, Sir, deceive me in this manner? I have followed you from Baden-Baden, and here I've had to climb 10,000 feet above the level of the sea after you. Henceforth you and I are strangers.

CHIRPEY (*at* L. C., *indignantly*). Not a word against this noble young man! You don't know how he has distinguished himself (*goes to* EARL *of* O., *enters into explanation with him and goes up stage*).

DR. M. (*looking all round*). And where is Harold? (*looks into cabin*.)

CENTLIVRE. Just like my ill fortune! Had they been a minute earlier, Harold would have lost this chance.

Lights down. The clouds disappear from the face of the moon. FRANCOIS *and* GUIDES *fully equipped with knapsacks, axes, &c., begin to ascend the* 2ND GLACIER R—*cutting steps in the ice as they go, and each with a lighted lantern strapped on to his back. They are all linked together by a rope tied round their waist, and with a short distance between each of them. Then* HAROLD *appears attached by the same means to the* GUIDE *preceding him. After him comes* FLORENCE, *and then* LORD SILVERSPOON—*each united to the other in a similar manner.*

Lime-light is thrown full upon them, and when they are half-way up the incline they halt to wave their "Adieux" to the characters grouped on the stage.

DR. M. (*down R.*) Where is Harold, I say? Harold!

EARL OF O. (*down L., with a polite bow, and pointing to* HAROLD). See him there, Doctor! My son I am sure will only be too happy to give way to yours.

CENTLIVRE (*aside*). I'll win the girl yet!

CHIRPEY (*seizing the enormous cow-herd's horn*). Hurrah! There they go! And now to give 'em a tune on this musical caterpillar (*blows horn*).

CHEERS *and* TABLEAU!

END OF ACT II.

ACT. III.

AT THE MARKET-PLACE OF CHAMOUNI.

SCENE.—*The Market-place at Chamouni.*

The cloth at back represents chain of mountains with their peaks covered with snow. Immediately in front of this is a "row" of the houses at the back of the market-place, and reaching to L. C.

On L. side, the wings are closed in with "built-up" houses. The first of these is the SYNDIC's *house, or rather Châlet, with broad projecting eaves. It has a "practicable" balcony in front of the upper story, and a flight of rude steps, with wooden balusters at side, parallel with the house front, and leading up to raised doorway—which is "practicable," and over which is printed "*BUREAU DE LA POLICE*." The next house is a Châlet for the sale of Swiss carvings and knick-knacks, with specimens hanging against the door-posts; and beyond this, perspective view of street—L. U. E. is left open.*

On R side, the wings are also closed in from 4th to 2nd E. Between 1st and 2nd grooves are two gate-posts, with railed gate thrown back between them, and lamp hanging above, on which is painted the words " Le Lion d'Or." Beyond this is the street front of the Hotel (the Scene to ACT I *having been that of the planted court-yard, or "hof" of the same) with "practicable" balcony to the upper story, and wooden colonnade "built-out" to the lower one. Beyond this again are other Châlet-like houses, with gables to the market-place. R. U. E. is left open, so as to admit of entrances being made (as on opposite side) from the upper corner of the " Place."*

In centre of stage, in a line with 3rd E, is a large rude stone-fountain, with streams of water flowing from the jets, and with steps leading up to the basin.

*The stage is covered with a cloth representing rude, knobbly paving stones, on which there are spread out, in front of the houses, collections of crockery-ware, tubs and pails, vegetables, cheeses, &c., for sale; and there is a stall at R. for poultry, butter, &c., and another at L. set out with fruit, flowers, &c.—the time of the " action" being supposed to be the "*THURSDAY'S MARKET.*"*

Projecting from the balconies of the Hotel are flags of the English, American, French, German, and Swiss colours, while that of the Syndic's house has a display of bright-coloured carpets and hearth-rugs hanging over the rails.

Previous to the rising of the curtain, firing of guns, pealing of bells, and huzzaing of the people are heard.

On the rising of the curtain, PEASANTS *are discovered filling their pails at the basin of the fountain, and market-people in front of their wares, pressing the passers-by to purchase. There is a crowd of* TOURISTS *and* VILLAGERS *assembled in the balconies of the Hotel and Syndic's house, and groups of* COUNTRY-PEOPLE *with the* WIVES AND CHILDREN OF GUIDES, *collected in the* MARKET-PLACE—*all staring off in direction of* L. U. E.

In front of the gate of the "Lion d'Or," R., WAITERS *are grouped. On R. side are* M. *and* MME. LAVIGNE, *the former with a small telescope in his hand, while the* TOURISTS *in the balcony of hotel have mostly "field-glasses" to their eyes.* FRITZ *is perched on top of the steps leading to door of* SYNDIC'S *house at L.*

General cheering, firing of guns, and pealing of bells, as the curtain goes up.

M. LAVIGNE (*at* R., *excitedly*). Here they come! I can see them just at the end of the bridle-road across the fields.

MME. LAVIGNE (*at* R.). It's scarcely eight hours since we fired the gun to mark they'd gained the summit.

Enter 2ND GUIDE, *running from* L. U. E. *to* L. 1 E.

2ND GUIDE. All's well! (*renewed cheers*) This makes the ninth time I've stuck my bâton on top of Mont Blanc! (*kisses wife and takes child up in his arms*).

FRITZ (*up steps,* L., *waving his napkin excitedly over his head*). Dey go to come! I see dem on de bridge!

MME. LAVIGNE (*to* FRITZ). Quick! run and call Monsieur Sheerpey and the rest of the party.

Exit FRITZ *by hotel-gates,* R. 1 E.

M. LAVIGNE. It's more than an hour since they came on ahead.

Enter TOWN CRIER, *down steps,* L. U. E.

TOWN CRIER (*to* MOB). Stand back there! They arrive!

M. LAVIGNE (*to* 2ND WAITER). Bring out the tribute that the "Golden Lion" offers to its brave *voyageurs*.

Exit 2ND WAITER *by hotel-gates,* R. 1 E.

TOWN CRIER (*coming down* L., *to children of* GUIDES). And you, girls, get ready your bouquets, and remember your curtseys.

Enter CHIRPEY *running on* R. 1 E. *He has discarded the costume he wore in* ACT II., *and appears in every-day dress.*

CHIRPEY (*excitedly, waving his handkerchief*). Bravo! let's give her a good reception! (*goes* L. C. *and looks round*) Halloa! they haven't got here yet! (*wiping his head with his handkerchief*) How I ever got down from those Mulets to *terra firma*, Fate and the Guides only know. The last lucid idea of "yours truly" upon the matter is that of having placed his person on a buttered slide at a sharp gradient, and that, after performing as many evolutions in the air as a tumbler pigeon, this unfortunate bit of goods was conveyed express to a very abrupt terminus—the wrong side up, with care. As for my poor dear spouse, she went rolling and rolling away down the mountain-side, with her body and clothes in such a tangle that it was as difficult with her, as it is with a skye terrier, to distinguish one extremity from the other. (*cheers heard without*) Now, then, clear the course there! Get out of the way, you young 'uns! (*jumping about with delight*) Here comes my Florence! She's been and done "Mont Blanc"—as slick as a squirrel mounts a tree!

Enter Mrs. Chirpey *and* Miss Jetsam, R. 1 E., *in other costumes than those worn in* Act II., *and followed by* 2nd Waiter, *who brings out round table set out with fruits, flowers, and champagne, and places it by first pillar of hotel-gates,* R.

Mrs. C. Where is she? Poor girl! she must be dead by this time—if she is anything like her dear mother.

(Band *without.*)

(*Cheers without.*) Town Crier *clears a passage.*

Chirpey (*crossing to and shaking* Mrs. C.). Wake up, old lady! Here they are! (*gets* R.)

Enter Procession, *with* Florence, Harold M., *and* Lord S., L.U.E. *in the following order.—It crosses behind fountain, and goes down* R. *to* L.

1. Town Official *bearing flag.*
2. Town Fiddler *and* Piper *playing a march.*
3. *Four of principal* Guides *bearing ice-axes.*
4. Florence, *with* Harold M. *on one side, and* Lord S. *on the other.*
5. *Rest of* Guides *with* Families *carrying axes, ropes, and lanterns.*
6. Boys *and* Girls *carrying hampers and bâtons of ascending party.*
7. Porters *and* Volunteers *carrying knapsacks and cooking utensils.*
8. Villagers *and* Peasants *bearing green boughs.*

(Band *plays.*)

As the procession comes down the stage, bells peal, crowd cheers, and people in balconies wave handkerchiefs and hats.

During the entry of the procession Chirpey *is being restrained with difficulty by* Town Crier *from breaking through the ranks and rushing up to* Florence.

Girls *come forward from* R., *and, curtseying formally, present bouquets to* Florence, Harold M., *and* Lord Silverspoon, *amid general cheering.*

Chirpey (*at* R., *wedged in by* Crowd, *and bursting away from* Town Crier, *as he pushes on one side the* Girls, *who are in the act of presenting flowers*). Hang it! are a father's feelings to be bottled up by a town-crier? (*lifting Florence off the saddle and throwing his arms round her neck as he hugs her to him*) Florence, my darling! (*then bursting into tears*) I never felt so happy in all my life. (*then indignantly to* Mrs. C.) And *you*, you fond old fool of a mother, would have stopped the girl from letting the world see the indomitable pluck of the Chirpey family.

Florence (*at* C.). Yes, Daddy; we've triumphed over Mont Blanc! But a hard-won battle it has been. On we marched, in the dead of night, amid the stillness of the tomb and the solitude of the desert, tramping along the boundless wilderness of eternal winter—where every footstep might open up a grave and every puff of wind bring down an avalanche to bury us. But up! up! up! we mounted! at one time staggering along in our struggles with sleep, as though every sense were drugged with drowsiness—at another, halting to gasp for breath, while each gasp seemed to tear the lungs from the chest with the agony of breathing.

MRS. C. *crosses to* FLORENCE *at* C., *kisses her, and goes back to* R. C.

HAROLD M. (*at* L. C.). But once on the summit, with our feet upon the conquered monarch's head, it made all our hearts leap to see the air of triumph with which Miss Florence planted her batôn in the snow, and to hear the silver-clarion tones of glory with which an English girl could cry, "Victory! Victory!"

FLORENCE (*laughing*). But you should have seen, Dad, the struggle to get to the winning-post—oh! it was as exciting as a steeplechase. And Baptiste, the Guide here, will tell you that, when the numbers were run up at the finish, it was—that promising filly, *Miss Florence*, ONE (*bowing to people*); *Mr. Harold*, the favourite, and previous winner, TWO (*bowing to* HAROLD M.); and the thoroughbred yearling, *Lord Silverspoon*—a "bad third" (*bowing to* LORD S., *at* L.).

2ND GUIDE (*at* L.). And, what's more, Ma'm'selle has been up higher than any of *us*; for on the summit I lifted her up in my arms, so that the victory on her part might be above all. (*Cheers.*)

M. LAVIGNE *approaches with a bottle of champagne, and* MME. LAVIGNE *with a plate of fruit from gates* R.

HAROLD M. (*waving his hand*). No, no! we need other refreshment. Keep that for the Guides' Banquet this evening. (*Renewed cheering.*)

BAND *strikes up.*

Exeunt CROWD *and* GUIDES, L. U. E. *and* R. U. E., *and* CHIRPEY, MRS. C. *and* FLORENCE *with* MISS JETSAM, HAROLD M. *and* LORD S., *followed by* M. *and* MME. LAVIGNE, *and* WAITERS, *into hotel,* R.

Some of the MARKET-PEOPLE *pack up goods and go off* R. U. E.

MARKET-WOMAN, *who has been walking about the stage since the commencement of the Act, goes over to hotel-gates* R. *with basket of butter and eggs on her head, and rings at gate-bell, when*

Enter FRITZ R. 1 E.

FRITZ *proceeds to chaffer with her for the purchase of some of the articles, and while this is going on,*

Enter CAPTAIN BROADSIDE, R. U. E. *He comes down* L. C.

CAPTAIN B. I've found the very spot for this duel. (*to* FRITZ) Here, Fritz!

(FRITZ *advances with the butter which he has bought on a platter, and which he keeps tasting in a critical manner.*)

Give my compliments to Mr. Chirpey, and say Cap'n Broadside desires to speak with him—(*significantly*) out here!

FRITZ (*as he samples the roll of butter with his finger-nail and smacks his lips approvingly*). Vare goot, Monsieur!

Exeunt FRITZ *and* MARKET-WOMAN, R. 1 E.

CAPTAIN B. I've paced the ground, and they can pick each other off (*imitating the action of duelling with pistols*) as comfortably as we used to pot the pirates in the Malacca Straits.

Enter CHIRPEY, R. 1 E.

CHIRPEY (*talking off indignantly at* R.). No! I'm jiggered if I do! If the sun *has* taken the skin off her nose, tell Mrs. Chirpey to cold-cream *herself*.

Act III. MONT BLANC. 49

CAPTAIN B. Don't excite yourself, Sir! You've got to fight a duel with that pugnacious parched-pea of a Frenchman in the morning. I hope you'll behave like a man, Sir.

CHIRPEY (*indignantly*). I fight a duel! Do you think I'm going to behave like an ass?

CAPTAIN B. (*in a towering rage*). What the devil do you mean, Sir? You're pledged to fight, and you *shall* fight. If you won't fight the Frenchman, may I be keelhauled, Sir, if you shan't fight *me!*

CHIRPEY (*aside in despair*). Well, as it's Hobson's choice about fighting some one, I'll let the old fire-eater there believe I'll have a crack at Mounseer.

CAPTAIN B. Well, Sir; you'll remember I've arranged with the Professor to be on the ground early to-morrow. Place of meeting— Forest of "Les Pélerins" at the back of the Pavilion; weapons—pistols; time—six a.m.; distance—twelve paces. (*goes up* L. C.) I shall now leave you to put your affairs in order, and will go in search of the shooting irons and the doctor.

Exit CAPTAIN BROADSIDE, L. U. E.

CHIRPEY (*dismally at* C.) The shooting irons and the doctor! (*shuddering*) Eugh! (*then with a knowing wink*) *I* fight a duel? "Do you see any green about me?" as my pickles said to the analytical chemist. Still, how to get out of it? (*pondering*.)

Enter CENTLIVRE, R. 1 E. *He goes up* R., *then crosses behind fountain and comes down* L. C.

Oh, here's Percy! (*still pondering*) Let me see! which will be the best way to work *him* (*pretends not to notice* CENTLIVRE, *and goes meditating up to one of the stalls, at* R., *where he is seen to examine the game and poultry exposed for sale, and to do so as if still revolving something in his mind.*)

CENTLIVRE. There he is. The nail must be clenched to-day or never.

Enter HAROLD *and* FLORENCE (*in every-day costume*), R. 1 E.

HAROLD M. (*as entering.*) And you really mean to tell me that after all your late exertions you don't feel in the least "done up"?

FLORENCE (*crossing to* L.) "Done up," Mr. Majoribanks? Not I Nor am I the craft to throw out signals of distress when I've only just got aground. But I want your assistance in the selection of some grapes for poor dear Mama.

HAROLD M. Ha! ha! *vous avez raisins, Ma'amselle?*

(*They retire up stage* L. *and then come down and stop at fruit-stall, inspecting the different articles.*)

CENTLIVRE (*catching sight of* HAROLD *and* FLORENCE). Soh! a false move now, and I'm checkmated. My queen's in danger! This duel—that chattering Frenchman couldn't keep to himself—may be of advantage to me.

CHIRPEY (*coming down from stall* R., *and talking to keeper of it*). No! I don't want it! (*aside*) I've got a brilliant thought.

CENTLIVRE *to* CHIRPEY (*coming down from* R. C.) Hush! I know all, and I honour your courage, Sir!

CHIRPEY (*with pretended bravery*). Sir, when the trumpet sounds to arms, do you think Chirpey cares?—no! (*heroically*) not one brazen blast! You shall *not* stop this duel!

FLORENCE *starts at the word "duel," and, drawing close to the fountain, listens attentively.*

E

CENTLIVRE. Let me, I beg of you, Sir, play the part of the dove, and be the bearer of the olive branch.

CHIRPEY. You don't know me, Sir. Though by nature mild as a vegetarian, still this body, when swollen with sanguinary intentions, becomes converted into a black pudding of the darkest dye (*melo-dramatically*)—so full it is of blood (*takes stage* R.).

MARKET-WOMAN (*down* R. C., *bringing a plucked bird from the stall, and thrusting it into* CHIRPEY's *hand as he waves it heroically at the end of the preceding speech*). Have it at your own price. It's quite fresh. Shot early in the morning.

CHIRPEY (*letting fall the dead bird*). Shot early in the morning. Eugh! how cold it feels!

MARKET-WOMAN *picks up bird and offers it a second time*. CHIRPEY *puts his hands behind him, shakes his head, and crosses to* R. C. MARKET-WOMAN *retires to stall* R.

CENTLIVRE (*aside*). Enough! I understand (*crosses behind to* R.) And now to write to the Police. *Exit* CENTLIVRE, R. 1 E.

FLORENCE (*excitedly, as she brings* HAROLD M. *forward*). Mr. Majoribanks, I need your aid. I've overheard all. This way, and I will tell you.

HAROLD M. (*aside as going off*). Centlivre can never have been playing me false with the father! No! no! Percy's above *that*, I'll swear. (*Offers his arm to* FLORENCE.)

Exeunt FLORENCE *and* HAROLD M. *into Châlet*, L.

CHIRPEY. I'm afraid I did'nt put it strongly enough to him. So, to make matters doubly safe, I'll write to the Police myself (*takes out a note-book and proceeds to write in it, sitting down at table* R). It 'ud never do to pen the letter in the Hotel. It might leak out that *I* had sent it (*as he writes*). "*To the Superintendent of Police. Sir,—It is my duty to inform the authorities that two blood-thirsty individuals purpose shooting one another to-morrow morning at a quarter to six*"— (It's better to make it a quarter of an hour earlier to them, so that they may be in time)—"*at a quarter to six, in the Forest of Les Pélerins, at the back of the Pavilion.*" (They can't make any mistake about *that!*) "*As a disinterested party, and a member of the Peace Convention of Geneva,*"—(the Peace Convention's quite an artistic touch—shows such a fine moral motive, you know, for writing the letter,)—"*I appeal to you to interpose the strong arm of the law, and have Captain Achille Fortinbras conveyed to the nearest dungeon, and kept in irons as a monster dangerous to society.*" (*Tears leaf out of book, folds it up, and directs it.*)

Enter FRITZ, R. 1 E.

FRITZ *goes to fruit stall* L., *and is seen to be purchasing a melon, while, as he haggles with the fruit-woman, he keeps on tasting the different kinds of fruit*.

CHIRPEY (*as he tears the sheet out of his note book, folds it up, and directs it*). There! that's off my mind! (*shows letter*) But who's to take it? (*goes over to* L., *is about to speak to* FRITZ, *but sees* CENTLIVRE R. *Retires up* L).

Enter CENTLIVRE, *with letter concealed in his hand*, R. 1 E.

CENTLIVRE. I've acted on Mr. Chirpey's hint, and this (*showing letter*) is sure to get him arrested to his heart's content. But who's to take it? (*goes up* R).

Act III.   MONT BLANC.   51

Enter HAROLD M. *from Châlet* L. *He comes down* C. *with letter concealed in his hand.*

HAROLD M. (*up* C.) I have done as Florence wished! (*shows letter.*) This will put a stop to Captain Fortinbras' little game. But who's to take it? (*goes up stage looking* R. *and* L.)

FRITZ (*coming down from stall* L. *to* C. *with his hands full of his purchases*). *Magnifique dessert* for de banquet of de Guides dis evening (*keeps on eating plums, grapes, &c.*)

CHIRPEY (*at* L.) }
CENTLIVRE (*at* R.) } (*coming down and perceiving* FRITZ). Ah, here's Fritz!
HAROLD M. (*up* C.) }

CHIRPEY (*about to give letter to* FRITZ *and concealing it hurriedly*). Mustn't let *them* see it? (*down* L. *and then up* L.)

CENTLIVRE (*down* R. *and then up* R. *about to give letter to* FRITZ *and concealing it hurriedly*). Mr. Chirpey here! he'll think the more of it, if I keep it dark from him.

HAROLD M. (*down* C. *and then up* C. *about to give letter to* FRITZ *and concealing it hurriedly*). Florence enjoined me to secresy.

The three saunter about in an apparently unconcerned manner.

FRITZ (*at* C.) Make vare goot business! Raisins vare goot market! (*dropping a grape into his mouth and smacking his lips after it.*) Smack me vare delica-at!

HAROLD M. (*aside as he beckons* FRITZ *over to* R. C.) Here, Fritz, take this to it's address at once—very urgent! and there's a franc for you (*gives letter and money and goes up* C.)

FRITZ (*looking at the money*). Goot!

CENTLIVRE (*calling* FRITZ *over to* R.). Fritz! (*then aside to him*) Take this to its address at once—very urgent! and here's a two-franc piece for you (*gives letter and money, and goes up* R.)

FRITZ (*looking at the money*). Ah, dat ist besser!

CHIRPEY (*calling* FRITZ *to* L.). Here, waitah! You'll excuse my helping myself to a grape (*drops letter in the basket as he plucks a grape off one of the bunches; then aside to* FRITZ). Take that to its address at once—very urgent! (*then, aloud*) and here are five francs for you! (*goes up* L.)

HAROLD M. (*as he comes down* R. C. *puts his fingers to his lips, and then says aside to* FRITZ *on leaving, as he plucks him by the sleeve*). Sh-sh!
Exit HAROLD M., R. 1 E.

CENTLIVRE (*down* R. *and aside to* FRITZ *on leaving*). Sh-sh!
Exit CENTLIVRE, R. 1 E.

CHIRPEY (*going to* FRITZ L. C.) Dear me! what a remarkably-fine flavour (*takes another, crosses* R., *and then to* FRITZ *with his mouth full*) Sh-sh!
Exit CHIRPEY, R. 1 E.

FRITZ (*counting up the money in his hand*). H-m, vare goot business! But, vhy-for, sh-sh! sh-sh! sh-sh! (*imitating each of them. Then, as he reads addresses on the three letters*). To de Gommissaire of Bolice! Gommissaire of Bolice! Gommissaire of Bolice! H-m! great cry for Bolice! I take dem to the Syndic here! (*pointing to* L. 1 E., *and then, as moving off*). Dwo steps for eight franc! H-m! Vare goot market!

Exit FRITZ, *up steps into* SYNDIC'*s house* L.

LORD S., *during the preceding scene, has entered from* R. 1 E., *and, having crossed the stage, after walking leisurely about the market, and buying a peach at the fruit-stall, has gone into the Swiss knick-knack shop,* L. 2 E.

E 2

Enter LORD S. *from shop*, L. 2 E., *with his hands full of carved toys.*

LORD S. There's the lovely Jetsam (*sees her on balcony,* R. 2 E., *and kisses his hand to her on tip-toe*). Miss Jetsam, I've something for you. Come down, my poppet. (MISS J. *disappears.*) I meant to have bought the girl a Geneva watch, and I should too, but my pocket-money wouldn't run to it.

Enter SYNDIC L. *He comes down steps, reading one of the letters, and throws up his hands as he goes off hurriedly* L.U.E. *He is followed by* FRITZ, *who goes off* R. 1 E.

Enter MISS JETSAM, R. 1 E.

MISS J. (*at* R.) Oh, my Lord! I haven't seen you since your triumphal entry into the village.

LORD S. (*at* L., *arranging his shirt-collar and cuffs*). Ye-es. I rather think that was a matter to be proud of. But Chirpey, you know, spoilt the business. He's a very good fellah, but of course one can't expect such people to have the feelings of gentlemen.

MISS J. What do you mean, Sir? Mr. Chirpey is the best friend I ever had in the world. Look here, my Lord, that man took me to his home when I was left a waif and stray—utterly destitute in the world. My mother happened to have been the teacher of his daughter. Florence and I grew up at school as sisters together; and, when my poor mother died penniless and left me a mere child without a home, Mr. Chirpey took me to his hearth and heart, (*then with scornful indignation,*) and how dare you, Sir, tell me that such a man has not the feelings of a gentleman?

LORD S. (*bowing*). I beg your pardon! I am but a boy, and we boys often talk without thinking. Had I known this before, I should have respected Mr. Chirpey as much as you do. So let us make it up once more and cement the reunion with a basket of peaches (*as they go up stage* L.) I've noticed some plummy ones up here.

They retire up stage, saunter about, and then exeunt R. 1 E. *while the following scene is going on, but before the gendarmes enter.*

Enter PROFESSOR WINDBEUTEL, *and* DR. MAJORIBANKS, *followed by* CHIRPEY, R. U. E. *They come down stage to the front of fountain.*

Enter CAPTAIN BROADSIDES, L.U.E. *He comes down* L. *quickly to* CHIRPEY.

CAPTAIN B. (*slapping* CHIRPEY *on the back*). Sir, I've got a bit of good news for you.

CHIRPEY (*brightening up suddenly*). No! have you though? What is it?

CAPTAIN B. (*looking round with great circumspection, and then in a half whisper*). I fancy this affair has got wind, and that some sneaking scoundrel has been writing to the authorities.

CHIRPEY (*with affected incredulity*). You don't say so! How abominable!

CAPTAIN B. (*slapping him on the back*). So, to make all safe, I've arranged to bring the matter off immediately.

CHIRPEY (*horrified*). Indeed! How kind!

DR. M. (*hurriedly*). Yes! all's prepared, I've got my instruments ready, and we've got a conveyance hard-by to take you off to the ground at once.

ACT III.   MONT BLANC.   53

CHIRPEY (*sinks on to the steps of the fountain L. C., and others group round him*). The duel to come off at once! Then my letter to the police will be of no use. Oh, Christopher! you're a dead man.

Enter TWO GENDARMES, *L. U. E., rapidly. They pass at the back of the fountain and exeunt into hotel, R. 1 E. They are unnoticed by the party.*

CHIRPEY (*faintly*). But, Captain, don't you think—the matter might be settled by means of an uncompromising—of course uncompromising—apology?

Enter CAPTAIN FORTINBRAS *between the two* GENDARMES, *R. 1 E. They are unseen by all but* CHIRPEY, *who, as he sits on the fountain steps, has his face turned in the direction of the hotel.* CAPTAIN FORTINBRAS *struggles to get to the* PROFESSOR, *but is restrained by* GENDARMES, *and hurried off gesticulating, L. U. E.*

CAPTAIN B. Apology! what? *I* let *you* ap›logize, sir?
CHIRPEY (*who has watched and gloated over* CAPTAIN FORTINBRAS' *arrest, rises, rubs his hands with glee, draws himself up, and dilates his figure with an air of extreme dignity*). I apologize! (*aside, as he comes down*) Not now Mounseer is safe; (*and then with great indignation*) *I* apologize! Sir, in the hour of danger Chirpey is no longer flesh and blood but—bronze. (*He strikes a statuesque attitude*).

They all come forward.

CAPTAIN B. Come, Sir! we can lose no more time cooling our heels here.

Enter tall GENDARME, *L. U. E. He comes and places himself behind* CHIRPEY, *unperceived by him.*

CHIRPEY (*aside, as he rubs his hands gloatingly*), It was that touch about the Peace Convention did it! (*to the others with a warlike air*) Lead on to the field, gentlemen!

CHIRPEY *is about to move off majestically R. with* CAPTAIN B., PROFESSOR W., *and* DOCTOR M., *when he is quietly touched on the shoulder by* GENDARME, *who intimates in pantomime that* CHIRPEY *must go with him, L.*

CAPTAIN B. What the devil's this? Arrested! And I was looking forward to such a pleasant afternoon.

Exit CAPTAIN B., *R. U. E.*

PROFESSOR W. Ach a! ach! It makes me much heart-smarting—on mine honour-vort—the Herr with the Bolicemens so gaptivated to find.

Exit PROFESSOR W., *R. U. E.*

DR. M. (*at R.*) I'm sorry, Mr. Chirpey, that I can be of no service to you now. (*bowing*) Good afternoon to you. (*then, as about to exit*) Tut! tut! what a pity! when I wanted to have looked further into the diagnosis of gun-shot wounds.   *Exit* DR. M., *R. 1 E.*

CHIRPEY *walks up and down dejectedly. The* GENDARME (*who should be very tall*) *follows close at his heels very stolidly. After a turn or two—in the course of which he has looked occasionally behind him slily*—CHIRPEY *makes a faint attempt at a bolt, and is immediately collared by the official at R.*

CHIRPEY (*dejectedly*). No! it's no good! No chance of leg-bail with a great stork upon stilts like that after one (*turns round and looks the*

GENDARME *up and down.* GENDARME *touches him on the shoulder, and intimates by pointing off that* CHIRPEY *must go with him*). Lead on! you attenuated military spectre! (*as going off*) Mrs. Chirpey is right! —as the women always are in the long run. Harold *is* the better man of the two!

Exeunt CHIRPEY *and* GENDARME L. U. E.

Enter FLORENCE *hastily. She crosses to* L., HAROLD M. *following*—R. 1 E.

FLORENCE (*to* HAROLD M. *as entering*). Oh Mr. Majoribanks! The Doctor has just told me they've taken my poor dear father off to prison! What have you done?

HAROLD M. (*astonished*). *I*, Miss Florence? Why I directed the authorities to seize Captain Fortinbras.

FLORENCE. But nobody knew of the duel but you and me, and (*hesitating*)—Oh, yes! Mr. Centlivre. Ah! *he*, then, must have been the cause of it.

Enter MRS. CHIRPEY, *wildly followed by* MISS JETSAM, R. 1 E.

MRS. C. (*throwing herself on* FLORENCE'S *shoulder*). What have I heard? My Christopher taken to jail like a common pickpocket! I can see him now in a pepper-and-salt tight-fitting suit, picking oakum, with a loaded blunderbuss to his ear! One of my violent attacks is coming on! Run, Miss Jetsam, and fetch that darling Doctor Majoribanks, or I shall fall through the paving stones! (MISS JETSAM *is about to hasten off* R., *when*,

Enter DR. MAJORIBANKS, *hurriedly*, R. 1 E.

DR. M. (*crossing to* C.) I'm afraid, my dear Madam, the abrupt manner in which I communicated the sad intelligence to you has superinduced a shock to the system, which, supervening on the complication of organic derangements from which we are suffering, has brought about a reflex action of the motory nerves. (*feels her pulse*) H-m! as I expected—thick and ropy.

MISS J. But what is to be done for poor Mr. Chirpey?

FLORENCE. Mr. Majoribanks (*to* HAROLD M.), have you no course to suggest? or, perhaps your father could advise?

DR. M. (*as he continues attending to* MRS. CHIRPEY). A stated amount of caution, money, or else bail for a definite sum, must be given. The bail must be that of some old-established resident.

Enter M. LAVIGNE *from gates* R.

HAROLD M. Oh, if that is all, Sir, the difficulty is easily overcome (*is going off* R. *but sees* LAVIGNE *at gates*). Ah, the very man! (*goes and speaks to him hurriedly, and then rushes with him up* R.)

HAROLD, *as he crosses the stage, waves his hand to* FLORENCE, *who returns the greeting with evident signs of joy*.

Exeunt HAROLD *and* LAVIGNE, L. U. E.

FLORENCE (*running over to* DR. M.). Oh, Dr. Majoribanks, I can't thank your son as I should wish for all these services of his to one I love so dearly!

DR. M. Miss Florence, I admire your nice sense of filial respect! (*aside*) Tut! tut! it's wonderful how that girl improves on acquaintance!

MRS. C. Yes, Doctor, she's a very good girl. Kiss me, Florence, dear! Your mother won't be with you long. The last two days' sufferings have reduced her naturally-fine figure to the thread-paper you behold.

ACT III.   MONT BLANC.   55

Enter CHIRPEY, HAROLD M., *and* M. LAVIGNE, L. U. E.

HAROLD M. (*rushing down the stage, waving his handkerchief above his head*). Hurrah! he's free! Monsieur Lavigne here has, at my request, become security for his keeping the peace.

MRS. C. (*wildly*). Where is he? Let me fold him in my arms! (*hugs him to her, and looks first at him, and then at his clothes*) Thank goodness! they didn't pepper-and-salt you.

Enter CENTLIVRE, *who, on seeing Florence shake hands with* HAROLD, *starts, and retires up stage.*

FLORENCE (*approaching* HAROLD *and the* LANDLORD, *and shaking them both by the hand*). You understand what that means, gentlemen? It's better than words.

CHIRPEY (*breaking away from his wife's caresses*). You're right, Florence! I owe my liberty to them. Give me your hand, Harold.

CENTLIVRE (*aside*). So it's Harold again, is it? This will never do! He remembers the service Harold did him. I'll see if I can't jog his memory with a sense of his own heroism to *me*.

CENTLIVRE *goes up* L. U. E.

Enter TOWN CRIER L. U. E.

CHIRPEY (*to* DR. M.). It's not the first time, Doctor, your son has done me a good turn; and, until this heart grows cold in Chirpey's bosom—he recollects the rest. I can't manage any fine phrases, you know.

CENTLIVRE *comes down with* TOWN CRIER, L. U. E. (*unobserved by the above characters*). CENTLIVRE *makes signs to the* CRIER *to stand on the steps of the fountain, places a paper in his hand, appears to read it over to him, and then retires behind the crowd of* MARKET-PEOPLE *who begin to gather about the* CRIER. *This goes on during the following speech.*

DR. M. (*still as if persuading himself to the notion*). Now, that's a very nice sentiment! A diamond in the rough—but still a jewel—sparkling with genuine good feeling.

TOWN CRIER *stands on steps of fountain* C., *rings his bell at a signal from* CENTLIVRE *in the background. The characters in the front of the stage turn round to listen,—with the exception of* CHIRPEY *and* HAROLD.

TOWN CRIER (*chopping up his speech, and emphasizing it as marked*). Oh, yes! This is to give *notice*—that the thanks of the people of *Chamouni* are due to a gentleman of the name of *Chirpey!*

CHIRPEY (*who has remained in close and affectionate conversation with* HAROLD, *springs forward at the mention of his name*). Eh! what's that?

TOWN CRIER. Who, at the imminent peril of his *life*—and with a courage seldom *equalled*—and never to be *surpassed*—rescued a fellow-traveller from a violent *death*—among the terrible crevasses of the Grands *Mulets.*

CHIRPEY (*proudly*). It's true!

TOWN CRIER. It is but right that the people of *Chamouni*—should publicly express their gratitude to *Mr. Chirpey, of London*—for his *heroic conduct*—to whom all *honour and praise are due!* (CROWD *cheers.*)

CHIRPEY (*rushing to* TOWN CRIER *and fumbling excitedly in his pockets as he goes*). Here, my good man, drink my health! (*then in his ear*) You haven't got a spare copy of that—have you? (CRIER *shakes his head.*)

Exit TOWN CRIER R. U. E. *followed by* CENTLIVRE *and* CROWD.

CHIRPEY (*hurrying over to* DR. M.). There's glory for you! (*then hastening away to* HAROLD) Town Council have done it evidently—admirably regulated town this! (*then rushing to* MRS. C.) Kiss me, my darling! a'n't you proud of me? (*bell rings without.* FLORENCE *is about to speak, but he stops her.*) Don't speak! he's at it again! (*listens till distant cheers have ceased.*) And, now, what were you going to remark, my dear? (*crosses to* FLORENCE.)

FLORENCE (*at* R.). Why, Dad, that to make the oration complete, there ought to be a werd or two added about the heroic conduct of Mr. Harold to *you*.

CHIRPEY (*at* L.). Eh? Oh, yes, certainly! But, if the town *does* admire one's gallantry, hang it that's no reason why they should be *surfeited* with it. (*Bell heard again, but more faintly, without.*) He's at it again! Human nature can't stand this—I *must* hear it once more!

Exit CHIRPEY *running off* R. U. E.

DR. M. Harold, give me your arm; I've a few purchases to make in the village, and I wish to talk to you seriously. Ladies, your obedient servant (*bows*).

HAROLD M. Now's my chance! I'll see if I can't soften him. He must be adamant indeed if Florence hasn't made *some* impression on him (*bows to ladies, and looks lingeringly at* FLORENCE).

Exeunt HAROLD *and* DR. M., L. U. E.

FLORENCE (*sighs*). Come, mother dear! let's get in. The best of the market's gone.

MISS J. (*archly*). Ay! there's nothing worth looking at now—is there, Florence?

MRS. C. My dear, if such honours had been heaped upon your father in London, they would have made him Lord Mayor; not that I should ever have survived the ninth of November, for *that* turtle and the loving-cup always make your dear mother feel so poorly.

Exeunt MRS. C., FLORENCE, *and* MISS JETSAM R 1 E.

Enter CHIRPEY *and* CENTLIVRE *arm in arm* R. U. E.

CHIRPEY *keeps pressing* CENTLIVRE'S *hand affectionately as they come down the stage.*

CHIRPEY. (*at* L.C). Percy, this is a proud moment for me! Ever since you owed your life to me, I've felt like a father to you (*shakes him warmly by the hand*).

CENTLIVRE (*aside at* R.C). The iron's hot! I'll bend it to my will. (*to* CHIRPEY) And my chief aspiration, Sir, is the honour of being regard-d as your son. I owe my life to you. You can endow that life with happiness.

CHIRPEY (*stopping suddenly as they walk arm in arm about the stage*). Can I? Tell me how.

CENTLIVRE. You've done me the honour, Sir, to take my hand. Give me your sanction to offer that hand to your daughter.

CHIRPEY (*aside*). Here's honour upon honour—An Earl's son, too! Won't the old woman want a straight waistcoat! (*to* CENTLIVRE) Percy, my cup was full before, but now (*wiping his eyes*) you've set it running over.

CENTLIVRE (*aside*) Oh, joy! Florence is mine! (*then with great exultation*) Now, Harold, who wins the battle?

CHIRPEY. You have my good wishes; but, as *I'm* not going to marry you, the party mainly interested in the matter ought to have *some* voice in it. So leave me to talk it over with my daughter. (*crosses to L.*)

CENTLIVRE. I leave you, Mr. Chirpey, to plead my cause. I couldn't have a better advocate.

Exit CENTLIVRE R. 1 E.

Enter FRITZ *with letter* R.U.E.

FRITZ (*giving letter*). From de Herr Gabitaine Proatsite.

Exit FRITZ R. 1 E.

CHIRPEY (*amazed after glancing at the letter*). What's this? (*sits at table* R.) That parched-pea of a Frenchman let loose again—out on his *parole*. Oh, lor'! oh, lor'! I'm not safe yet. (*then, after another glance at letter*) Now I begin to see it all. The fog I've been in is dispersing (*takes another look at the contents*). Mounseer vows vengeance—swears he'll have my blood still—says I've insulted his country by wanting to stick up my pickle-bill beside the name of his grand nation. But how came the fellow to know anything about my pickle-bill?

Re-enter HAROLD M. *from house* L.U.E.

I kept it a secret from every one but (*starts as he catches sight of* HAROLD M.) him (*rises*)—the very man who's done it all! (*crosses to him*).

HAROLD M. (*aside, at* L.) Alone! Now to put it to him plainly and straight-forwardly. (*to* CHIRPEY, *in a supplicating manner*) Sir, I've come to ask you——

CHIRPEY (*snappishly at* C). A favour, no doubt! I can see it in your face. Sir, I detest being asked to grant favours as much as I hate to receive them.

HAROLD M. (*at* L.C.) I beg of you, Mr. Chirpey, not to think of any service that I may have been fortunate enough to render you.

CHIRPEY (*at* R.C., *exultingly as he nurses his anger*). There, I knew it was coming; he rendered me a *service*; and now he comes—cap in hand—with his little account for past favours. Tit for tat, of course!

HAROLD *is about to explain*.

CHIRPEY (*going on railing*). Not a word, Sir. I guess your errand; you have come to ask me the greatest favour one man can bestow upon another.

HAROLD M. (*impulsively*), I have, Sir! and let me entreat you——

CHIRPEY. And that favour is to give you my child. (HAROLD *bows*.) I guessed as much! You saved my life, and therefore you believe you have a right to demand a recompense which is as dear as *life* to me.

HAROLD M. (*indignantly*). You misunderstand me, Mr. Chirpey!

CHIRPEY (*excitedley*). I don't. I've noticed it in your manner—your grand patronising air—ever since you *rescued* me. It has galled me, Sir—galled me! I would have you to know that Christopher Chirpey is a self-made man. He's climbed up the ladder—from a shop-boy to a merchant—from servitude to independence—without a helping hand. (*goes up* R.) He's never been under an obligation to anybody. (*with a faint shudder*). Can't bear the sense of it! and dam'me if he will!

Exit CHIRPEY (*fuming*) R. U. E.

HAROLD M. (*despairingly*). How little was I prepared for this! The angry storm has blown the bright mirage to the winds. Good-bye my hopes! Farewell, Florence! The girl is too good to act contrary to her father's wishes, and, thank Heaven, I'm not base enough to tempt her to oppose them. Come, Harold, rouse yourself! the world's open to you; go and staunch your wounds in the activity of work. Yet it's like tearing my heart-strings to leave her. The world's open to me it's true; but oh, Florence! Florence! open to me as a desert (*buries his face in his hands*).

Enter CENTLIVRE R. 1 E.

CENTLIVRE. What, Harold! (*slapping him on the back*) and in the dumps too! Well, well! I can guess what grieves you—you've lost the battle. Look here, Harold, I want to give you a bit of advice.

Enter CHIRPEY R. U. E., *sauntering down stage and fanning himself with his handkerchief. He takes a turn or two about the Market, and then retires behind the fountain* C.

Can't you see, that when you do a man a service, you place him under an obligation; and an obligation's a burden of the world which is so crushing that it wants a moral Atlas to bear up against it. Now, to state the case plainly, as regards yourself and Mr. Chirpey—

CHIRPEY *puts his head up over the fountain-basin* C.

although *he* can hardly be cited as an average type of the weakness of human nature; for the man's as vain as a peacock, and as easily caught as a booby!

CHIRPEY *suddenly disappears behind fountain* C.

Still, when you saved his life, you committed a grave indiscretion.

HAROLD M. Did I?

CENTLIVRE. Of course you did, old boy! You fancied that the recollection of the act would always recall to him a feat of deep devotion on your part.

HAROLD M. Pardon me, I fancied nothing of the kind.

CENTLIVRE. And what has been the consequence? Why, instead of being grateful to you, whenever you make your appearance, your presence humiliates him. He feels he is your "*obliged servant.*"

HAROLD M. But I never wanted him to feel like this.

CENTLIVRE. Now, on the other hand, just contrast your procedure in the contest with my own. I let myself slide accidentally—on purpose—into a small crevasse, which I need hardly tell you wasn't *very* deep nor *excessively* dangerous.

HAROLD M. On purpose?

CENTLIVRE. On purpose! For give a vain man the opportunity of displaying his courage by saving a fellow-creature—without danger to himself—and it is a master-stroke in social diplomacy.

HAROLD M. This is the old Jesuits' trick: the fair end justifying the foul means.

CENTLIVRE. And now for the result. Since that time I have been a glory to the man—a triumph. At sight of me his figure swells with pride—the peacock spreads his feathers.

HAROLD M. Is the lesson ended?

CENTLIVRE. One moment. Not only do I allow him the glory of believing he saved me; but I send the town-crier round to sing his praises.

HAROLD M. *You* sent the town-crier round?

CENTLIVRE (*bowing*). Yes! I purchased the trumpet of Fame—for the small sum of five francs. And so ends the fable.

HAROLD (*sarcastically.*) And have you no *moral* to it?

CENTLIVRE. I have! It is this: men do not attach themselves to us on account of the services we force upon *them*, but rather for those which we allow *them* to render *us*.

HAROLD M. And *this* you call diplomacy! I call it by a harsher but truer name—duplicity. *I* have always believed that the conduct of a gentleman should be distinguished by honour and plain-dealing. But *you*, Percy, would reverse the old proverb that "honesty's the best policy," and endeavour to teach me that *policy* is better than honesty. Well, *you*, Cent, are the successful diplomatist (*with a bow*). *I'll* be content to remain the humble gentleman.

CHIRPEY *saunters leisurely down L. to the front.*

CHIRPEY (*as if astonished at seeing them, and with well-suppressed rage*). Ah, Percy! Ah, Harold! what, you here? Nothing private eh? (PERCY *shakes his head and* CHIRPEY *crosses to* C.) I am glad to hear it; because you two gentlemen have both done me the honour to solicit the hand of my daughter in marriage. I've just been taking a stroll, and thinking the matter over. And, as I have no reason to be ashamed of my decision, and don't like anything *private*—why, I'll just call a few of my friends to hear it (*goes to gate-bell R. and pulls away at it violently—as if he were working off his rage—as he shouts*) Here Florence! Mrs. Chirpey! Miss Jetsam! Dr. Majoribanks! Come out! all of you.

Enter all the Characters—except CAPTAIN FORTINBRAS, PROFESSOR WINDBEUTEL, CAPTAIN BROADSIDE, FRITZ, *and* FRANCOIS—R. 1 E. *hurriedly. They group themselves round about* CHIRPEY, HAROLD, *and* CENTLIVRE—MRS. C. *crossing behind* CHIRPEY *and getting on his* L. *side.*

CHIRPEY (*at* C. *gravely*). Florence, come here! (*takes her by the hand*) You have two suitors for your hand—though I dare say you found *that* out long before I did. I am about to give you away to a gentleman in every way worthy of you. You can't tell, giddy girl (*chucking her under the chin*) how a father feels when the time comes for him to hand over the child he has cherished so long, to—to—(*bursts into tears, and buries his head on* FLORENCE's *shoulder*).

MRS. C. (*sobbing loudly at* L. C.) Boo-ooh!

CHIRPEY (*to* MRS. C. *as he starts up and wipes his eyes hurriedly*). You old fool! what are *you* blubbering about?

FLORENCE. You know, Daddy dear, your wish has always been law to me. But surely, at such a moment, *I* ought to be allowed some little——

CHIRPEY. There! there! how you women will gabble! Leave it to me! Percy, come here.

HAROLD M. All is lost then. (*goes up* C.)

FLORENCE. Oh, father!

CENTLIVRE (*aside, as he advances down* L. C. *and says exultingly to* HAROLD). I told you how it would go.

CHIRPEY. Percy, I am about to give you what I trust you will treasure for life.

CENTLIVRE (*with extreme deference*). Oh, Sir, words cannot——

CHIRPEY. I am about to give you—a piece of advice.

CENTLIVRE (*incredulously*). What?

CHIRPEY. And that is—never speak of private matters in public places.

CENTLIVRE (*with a groan*). He must have overheard me. (*goes up* L.)

CHIRPEY. (*at* R. C.) I'm not so utterly ungrateful, Sir, as you would make me out; I have at least gratitude enough to thank you for the lesson you have taught me. Harold, come here! although you calculate less than your friend, you please me more. Florence, you come here too. I shouldn't like to have to assert a father's prerogative, and *force* you to take this gentleman.

FLORENCE (*at* L. C. *with a bow of mock humility*). It is the aim, father, of every well-trained young lady to follow her parents' wishes.

DR. M. (*at* R., *as if putting it to himself argumentatively*). Now there's something about that little turn of sentiment which is excessively charming—*ex*cessively charming! Harold was right! she *is* a most fascinating creature, and in every way worthy of him.

EARL OF Q. (*at* L. *with a polite bow to* DR. M.). I told you so, Doctor. My son is only too happy you see (*pointing to* CENTLIVRE, *who looks the picture of misery*) to give way to yours.

CHIRPEY (*giving* FLORENCE *to* HAROLD). There, Harold, take this priceless gift as your recompense. Still don't believe by such a return I wish to get rid of a debt which will always make me glad to acknowledge myself (*with a look at* CENTLIVRE) your *obliged servant*.

HAROLD M. I won her, Sir, I fancy, in an honest, straightforward way; and in such a way we'll go through life together—won't we, Florence dear?

MRS. C. *My* daughter to be married to the son of one of our most eminent physicians! Oh, what a delightful prospect of advancement in life for my child, and of "advice gratis" for myself!

MISS J. (*aside, to* LORD S.). Now, my Lord, is Mr. Chirpey the gentleman at heart I told you he was?

LORD S. Ye-es! I'm glad, Miss Jetsam, to admit my error. (*coaxingly*) But, my darling, what's to become of us? Am I to be left out in the cold?—and without so much as a "comforter" about my neck?

MISS J. (*laughingly, as she turns away*). Oh, come along, do! (*They go off and are seen to come on Balcony* R.)

HAROLD M. (*going over to* CENTLIVRE, *who stands dejectedly, with his back turned towards the central figures*). Come, Percy! remember the terms of our agreement; the hand before the battle, and——(*pauses, as if waiting to see whether* CENTLIVRE *is disposed to take the hand which he extends to him*).

CENTLIVRE (*who gives outward signs of an inward struggle, and then, as if overcoming his feelings*). And *after* it too, Harold! (*they shake hands cordially together*) I begin to think diplomacy isn't so fine a science for a gentleman after all. Well, you've won the fight, Harold; but remember!—I'm the "best man!" (*sits* R.)

Enter CAPTAIN FORTINBRAS *and* PROFESSOR WINDBEUTEL *with* CAPTAIN BROADSIDE, L. U. E.

CAPTAIN B. (*coming down* C. *and slapping* CHIRPEY *on back*). Congratulate me, Sir! I've settled all about the duel.

CHIRPEY. Captain Broadside, Sir! you've prevented bloodshed.

CAPTAIN B. I *prevented* it! I've just arranged with the Professor to dodge the authorities here, by taking you both over into Italy, and letting you fight it out there. (*crosses behind to* R.)

PROFESSOR W. *Ja wohl!* In Italia de barole goes for nodding. (*goes up* L.)

CAPT. F. (*at* L.) Oui! oui! Zare we can quite com-for-taable make ze breeches of ze peace.

CHIRPEY (*crossing to* CAPTAIN F.) Sir, I am no longer a fool. There's a greater courage than that of fighting duels: the courage of acknowledging that you're in the wrong. If I've offended you, Captain, in

Act III.   MONT BLANC.   61

any way, I tender you my apology as cordially as I offer you my hand. (*They shake hands. The Frenchman wants to embrace* CHIRPEY, *but he declines in comic pantomime.* CHIRPEY *turns away, and* CAPTAIN F. *falls into the arms of* CAPTAIN B. *at* R. C., *who retires in extreme disgust. The Frenchman then, with a shrug of the shoulders, returns to the German at* L. *and embraces him.*)

FRITZ. (*coming from hotel-gates*). De banquet for de Guides is sairved. Mr. Sheerpie, you are neetet to take de share. (*aside, as he takes cake of soap out of his pocket*), and he shall take mine zoab also.

CHIRPEY (*fussily*). I remember! I promised to make them a speech. (*to all*) Come along!

They are about to proceed in the direction of the hotel-gates when gun is fired without.

CHIRPEY (*suddenly stopping, and driving all the characters back—excitedly*). Halt! It's François! He has it then! that's the signal agreed upon.

Enter FRANÇOIS, *running down* R. *from* L. U. E.

FRANÇOIS (*holding up the roll of the bill*). I've found the bill, Sir! I promised I wouldn't come down from the Mulets till I'd got it. (*crosses* R. *to* CENTLIVRE).

CHIRPEY (*overjoyed*). Give it to me! Christopher Chirpey isn't the man to go through all this mountain-climbing for nothing. (*to* MRS. C.) I'll tell you what I mean to be up to, my dear. You know what a determined character I am. I mean this bill of my delicious "Persuasive Pickle" to make a stir in the world yet. I'll have it up on that splendid commanding site if I die for it. (*pointing off to* MONT BLANC).

MRS. C. Oh, Christopher!—and when you know I'm so poorly

CHIRPEY. I will! I'm still, thank goodnesss, as lively as a two-year old, and so I mean to "do" Mont Blanc every night—aye! and to keep on doing it night after night—until I've thoroughly succeeded.

BAND, BELLS, *and* CHEERS.

MRS. CHIRPEY *falls into* CHIRPEY's *arms, and*

TABLEAU.

LaVergne, TN USA
15 July 2010
189673LV00008B/86/A